Dr Catherine Dawson has been a researcher and writer since the mid-1980s. She has taught research courses at university to undergraduate and postgraduate students, and to community groups. She has written extensively for academic journals on a wide range of subjects, including research methodology.

Other study skills titles from How To Books

Introduction to Research Methods
Dr Catherine Dawson

Basic Study Skills
Dr Catherine Dawson

Writing a UCAS Personal Statement
Julia Dolowicz

Writing Your Dissertation
Derek Swetnam and Ruth Swetnam

How to Write an Assignment
Pauline Smith

ADVANCED RESEARCH METHODS

Dr Catherine Dawson

Practical books that inspire

Constable & Robinson Ltd
55–56 Russell Square
London WC1B 4HP
www.constablerobinson.com

First published in the UK by How To Books,
an imprint of Constable & Robinson Ltd, 2013

A copy of the British Library Cataloguing in Publication Data is available from
the British Library

ISBN 978-1-8452-8513-5 (trade paperback)
ISBN 978-1-4721-1010-7 (ebook)

Printed and bound by CPI Group (UK) Ltd, Croydon, CR0 4YY

1 3 5 7 9 10 8 6 4 2

Contents

STAGE 2: PLANNING YOUR PROJECT

STAGE 3: CONDUCTING YOUR RESEARCH

STAGE 4: ANALYSING YOUR DATA

STAGE 5: REPORTING YOUR RESULTS

      Acting Ethically When Conducting Research   202
      Obtaining Funding and Ethics   204
      Treating Participants with Respect   205
      Ensuring Anonymity and Confidentiality   206
      Conducting Research that Involves Risk   206
      Summary   207

      Glossary of Terms   209
      References, Further Reading and Resources   221
      Bibliography   232
      Index   236

Preface

This book has been written for people who intend to carry out social research at an advanced level. It covers both qualitative and quantitative techniques and is suitable for researchers working in the fields of health, education, sociology, psychology and the humanities. It is aimed at the following groups of researchers:

- Master's students;
- doctoral students;
- research assistants and associates working in further, higher and adult education;
- researchers working for public and private organizations;
- researchers working for charitable and not-for-profit groups.

The book is divided into five stages that guide you through your project. The first stage helps you to think about your project in terms of the epistemological, philosophical, theoretical and methodological debates that underpin advanced social research. These topics can be complex and daunting, but the book presents them in a clear, user-friendly way that will enable you to think about these issues, generate ideas, develop aims and objectives, and move your project forward.

The second stage of the book provides practical information about costing the project, obtaining funding for advanced-level projects, collecting background information, choosing the appropriate research methods, understanding sampling techniques and preparing an advanced-level research proposal.

The third section provides information about conducting research and collecting data. This involves an in-depth discussion about how to use a variety of data collection methods, such as interviews, focus groups and questionnaires. It also provides practical and up-to-date information about recording and storing information (including data protection legislation) and advice about using the internet for social research (to gather information and as a research tool).

The fourth section of the book provides advice about analysing data, including qualitative techniques such as content analysis, thematic analysis and comparative analysis, and quantitative techniques that employ descriptive and inferential statistics. This section also includes important information about ensuring validity and reliability when collecting and analysing data, and knowing how to critique and interpret data. The last chapter in this section covers the topic of theory generation, which is an important task that needs to be undertaken by all advanced social researchers.

The final section of the book covers issues of dissemination, such as producing papers for conferences, writing journal articles, publishing online (including open access) and producing a thesis. It also offers practical advice for postgraduate students who need to attend an oral examination (a viva). The last chapter of this section discusses research ethics, and includes issues such as confidentiality, anonymity, ethical funding and carrying out research projects that involve risk.

A comprehensive 'Glossary of Terms' is provided at the end of the book to explain some of the more complex terms used in social research. The book concludes with further reading and resources relating to individual chapters and an extensive reading list for those of you who want to follow up any of the topics covered.

Dr Catherine Dawson has been a researcher for over twenty-eight years, working in the public, private and higher education sectors. She has obtained a Master's degree in social research and a doctorate in adult education, and has completed a variety of research projects over the years. These include topics such as public perception of change in higher education, the learning choices of adult returners, basic skills education for prisoners, student housing in the southeast and students' alcohol misuse.

Dr Dawson has designed and delivered research methods courses at universities and run research methods training courses for workers in the public, private and charitable sectors. She has also written extensively for academic journals and is the author of an *Introduction to Research Methods*, which is aimed at students and employees who are new to social research.

STAGE 1

THINKING ABOUT YOUR RESEARCH

1 Understanding the Epistemological Debate

All researchers and students who are working at an advanced level will need to understand the epistemological debate. This is because this debate influences the design of your research, the methodology that guides you, the research methods you choose, your data gathering and your ability to add to existing knowledge (and develop theory) when your research project is complete. If you understand the epistemological debate you will be less likely to form beliefs that lack justification and you will avoid claiming knowledge where it is possible only to hypothesize. This chapter guides you through the debate, providing a definition of epistemology and a description of the different types of epistemology. It goes on to illustrate how the epistemological position is related to theoretical perspective. This will enable you to think more about how these issues influence the design of your research project.

Understanding the Importance of Epistemology

Epistemology is a branch of philosophy concerned with the theory of knowledge. The word comes from the word '*episteme*', which is the Greek word for knowledge or understanding. It refers to what we accept as knowledge, how we know what we know and how belief is justified. If you are conducting research at an advanced level it is vital that you understand the epistemological debate for the following reasons:

- Epistemology is fundamental to thought, the acquisition of knowledge, the reliance on senses, the ability to reason, and the development of concepts, hypotheses and social theory.

- Epistemology is connected to theoretical perspective and methodological choice.

- Good research questions can be designed only when the epistemological debate is understood and the standpoint of the researcher made clear.

- Epistemology has an influence on the way that quality of method and quality of data analysis are demonstrated.

- Epistemology influences the relationship between the researcher and the participant/subject/object.

- Epistemology influences the way that the researcher communicates and interacts with the participant/subject/object and with their audience.

- Epistemology influences the type and method of theory generation and knowledge building (and the way it is disseminated).

Tip Don't confuse *epistemology* (concerned with the study of the nature of human knowledge and how it is acquired) with *ontology* (concerned with the nature and structure of the world and how it can be articulated).

Knowing About the Different Epistemologies

There are different types of epistemology that have been identified by philosophers and researchers over time. Those that are most relevant for you as an advanced researcher are summarized below (see 'References, Further Reading and Resources' at the end of this book to find out more about these epistemologies and others).

- *Social epistemology* positions knowledge and justified belief within a particular social and historical context. There are different strands within social epistemology. For example, some believe that knowledge and justification are linked to truth, whereas others believe that scientific facts are social constructions and, therefore, cannot make claims to truth and reality.

- *Feminist epistemology* is concerned with the way that gender influences our concept of knowledge. It refers to the way knowledge can be judged to be adequate and how research methodologies and methods can be assessed. It questions existing knowledge that has been developed from flawed research.

- *Pragmatic epistemology* challenges the distinction that researchers and philosophers make between theoretical beliefs and practical deliberations. The assumption is that scientific investigation can solve problems and provide insights, with an emphasis placed on consequences, practice and experience.

- *Naturalistic epistemology* attempts to identify how knowledge and justification are rooted in the natural world through a combination of traditional conceptual analysis and empirical methods. This approach emphasizes the application of methods, results and theories from the empirical sciences.

■ *Evolutionary epistemology* attempts to address questions about the theory of knowledge from an evolutionary point of view. It assumes that knowledge is constructed by an individual or group of individuals in order to adapt to their environment. The construction of knowledge helps with survival and is an ongoing process that happens on a biological, psychological and social level.

Exercise 1: Asking Epistemological Questions

Work through the following questions as this will help you to think about the epistemological issues that are relevant to your own research.

What is knowledge?

What are the conditions of knowledge?

What are the sources of knowledge?

How do we acquire knowledge?

Is it possible to have knowledge at all?

Why do we know some things and not know other things?

Does our knowledge represent reality as it is?

What is reality? Is there any such thing?

What is justification?

What are the sources of justification?

How are we to understand the concept of justification?

What makes justified beliefs justified?

Is justification internal or external to a person's own mind?

How can we differentiate truth from falsehood?

Why do we believe certain claims and not others?

Connecting Epistemology and Theoretical Perspective

Crotty (1998) highlights three epistemological positions and discusses these in terms of their relationship with theoretical perspective (and methodology: see Chapter 2). It is important to think about these connections early in your research as they will have considerable influence on the design of your research project (see Fig. 1).

Fig. 1: The Interrelationship of Epistemology and Theoretical Perspective (Source: adapted from Crotty 1998)

Epistemological Position	Theoretical Perspective
Objectivism	Positivism, post-positivism
Subjectivism	Postmodernism, structuralism, post-structuralism
Constructionism	Interpretivism (symbolic interactionism, phenomenology, hermeneutics), critical inquiry, feminism

Objectivism

Objectivism highlights the importance of empirical facts and explicit articulate statements. Reality exists independently of consciousness: objective knowledge can be obtained through deductive reasoning and the truth found through replicable observation. Human knowledge and values are objective: they exist and can be discovered.

Theoretical perspectives within this position include positivism (empirical sciences are the sole source of true knowledge) and post-positivism (although objective truth is there to be sought, the researcher can influence what is observed).

Subjectivism

Subjectivism suggests that there is no underlying truth and that reality is only what we perceive it to be. All knowledge is limited to experiences by the self and transcendent knowledge is impossible. Therefore, knowledge cannot be discovered as it is subjectively acquired and everything is relative.

Theoretical perspectives within this position include postmodernism (there is no single defining source for truth and reality beyond the individual); structuralism (human cultures can be understood in terms of their relation to larger structures and systems); and post-structuralism (meanings and intellectual categories are shifting and unstable).

Constructionism

Constructionism suggests that knowledge is constructed by scientists and not discovered from the world. The only reality that we know is that which is expressed by human thought. Meaning and knowledge are human constructions.

Theoretical perspectives within this position include interpretivism, such as symbolic interactionism (behaviour is explained in terms of how people interact with each other via symbols); critical inquiry (existing knowledge, assumptions and questions are examined, analysed and reflected upon); and feminism (a collection of ideologies and movements aimed at improving the rights and powers of women).

Tip Note the important distinction here between constructivism and constructionism. Crotty (1998) points out that constructivism is to do with the meanings that people make in their own minds (a person's view is unique and valid), whereas constructionism is to do with how we create and transmit meaning collectively (culture gives us a distinct view of the world).

The next chapter will help to illustrate how these epistemological positions and theoretical perspectives have an influence on methodological choices. For fuller definitions of theoretical perspectives and methodologies, see the 'Glossary of Terms' at the end of this book. See 'References, Further Reading and Resources' to continue with the debate outlined above.

Tip Make sure that you have not, unthinkingly, located yourself within a particular epistemological standpoint when an alternative standpoint may better suit your research problem. Inappropriate matching of an epistemological standpoint and a methodological position can lead to questionable research results, so it is important to spend time getting this right at the start of your project.

Summary

Epistemology is the branch of philosophy that is concerned with the theory of knowledge. It questions how we know what we know, how we come to form our beliefs and how these beliefs are justified. There are different types of epistemology, including naturalistic, social and feminist epistemologies, and within each of these there are various standpoints. When thinking about your own research you need to consider your epistemological position, as this will have an influence on your theoretical perspective and the methodology that you choose for your research.

The next chapter will enable you to think more about these relationships, helping you to understand the methodological debate and move towards choosing an appropriate methodology for your research.

2 Understanding the Methodological Debate

Now that you have been introduced to the epistemological debate it is important to increase your understanding of the methodological debate. This will help you to think about, and decide upon, the most appropriate methodology for your research. As we have seen in the previous chapter, your epistemological standpoint will have an influence on theoretical perspective and this, in turn, will have an influence on methodological choices.

This chapter helps you to think about choosing an appropriate methodology by providing a definition of the term, illustrating the connections between epistemology, theoretical perspective and methodology, and describing the methodologies that are appropriate for social research projects at an advanced level.

Defining Methodology

In its broad sense methodology is a guideline system or framework that is used for solving a problem. It includes practices, procedures and rules used by those involved in inquiry and covers issues such as the constraints, dilemmas and ethical choices within your research.

For those involved in advanced research, methodology also includes the theoretical analysis of these systems or frameworks, a critique of other frameworks and a careful analysis of the interrelationship between epistemological standpoint, theoretical perspective and methodology.

Tip Make sure that you do not mistake methodology for methods. Methodology is the overall framework that guides your research, whereas methods are the actual tools that you use to carry out your research.

Relating Methodology to Epistemology and Theoretical Perspective

As we have seen in Chapter 1, Crotty (1998) identifies three epistemological positions and discusses these in terms of their relationship with theoretical perspective. He then demonstrates how these have an influence on methodology. An understanding of these interrelationships will help you to think more about your methodology (see Fig. 2).

Fig. 2: The Interrelationship of Epistemology, Theoretical Perspective and Methodology (Source: adapted from Crotty 1998)

Objectivism →	positivism, post-positivism →	experimental research, survey research
Subjectivism →	postmodernism, structuralism, post-structuralism →	discourse theory, deconstruction
Constructionism →	interpretivism (symbolic interactionism, phenomenology, hermeneutics), critical inquiry, feminism →	ethnography, grounded theory, phenomenological research, heuristic inquiry, action research, discourse analysis, feminist research

Knowing About the Different Methodologies

Fig. 2 illustrates that there are different methodologies that are influenced by the epistemological position. These methodologies are described below. However, it is important to note that these are flexible (researchers within each approach can be positioned on a scale, from an extreme standpoint to a mild standpoint, for example). Also, it is possible to adopt a multiple or mixed methodology approach that is flexible and crosses the boundaries between certain compatible approaches (see Chapter 9).

Methodologies within the objectivist standpoint

As we have seen in Chapter 1, objectivism presumes that things exist as meaningful entities, independent of consciousness and experience, that they have truth and meaning in them as 'objects'. Two main methodologies within this epistemological standpoint are experimental research and survey research.

Experimental research

Commonly referred to as the 'scientific method', experimental research can be viewed as both a methodology and a method. This type of research seeks to add to knowledge through diligent inquiry that involves systematic and controlled testing to understand causal processes. Researchers manipulate one or more variables, controlling and measuring changes in other variables. They also examine data, reports and observations in the search for facts or principles.

Survey research

Survey research is used to collect data about thoughts, opinions, attitudes, behaviour and feelings. Respondents are asked a set of predefined questions using methods such as questionnaires or structured interviews (by mail, telephone, internet or face-to-face, for example). This methodology can be used for exploratory purposes, to test theory and to understand and describe a particular phenomenon.

Survey research uses samples that are representative of the larger population of interest so that generalizations can be made (see Chapter 10). Issues of correlation, causality, reliability and validity are extremely important to researchers using this methodology (see Chapter 19).

Methodologies within the subjectivist standpoint

Subjectivism rejects the notion of objective truth and also rejects the idea of meaning being generated by the interaction of subject and object (see 'Methodologies within the constructionist standpoint', below). Instead, subjectivists maintain that reality as related to a given consciousness is dependent on that consciousness. Two main methodologies within this epistemological standpoint are discourse theory and deconstruction.

Discourse theory

Discourse theory suggests that textual deep structures have a semantic rather than a syntactic character (the *meaning* of language rather than the *structure* of language). It seeks to determine the universal semantic meaning of a text and display that meaning in the form of concepts, propositions and paragraphs, for example, and their relationship to one another. Discourse theory is used to build on existing knowledge and is subject to continuous debate and argument. It does not seek to provide specific answers to a problem.

Deconstruction

Deconstruction can be seen as a literary criticism that questions traditional assumptions about certainty, identity and truth. It challenges fundamental conceptual distinctions or oppositions in texts (for example, nature and culture, speech and writing, mind and body). Deconstructive analysis seeks to restructure or displace the opposition: it is suspicious of established intellectual categories and sceptical of claims to objectivity.

Methodologies within the constructionist standpoint

Constructionism rejects the notion of an objective truth: there is no meaning without mind, meaning is constructed not discovered and people construct their own meaning in different ways. The main methodologies within this epistemological standpoint are ethnography, grounded theory, phenomenological research, heuristic inquiry, action research, discourse analysis and feminist research.

Ethnography

Ethnography is the study and systematic recording of human cultures and human societies. The emphasis in ethnography is on describing and interpreting cultural behaviour and phenomena. The world is observed from the point of view of the subject rather than the ethnographer. All behaviour is observed and recorded through fieldwork, although a distinction is made between everyday and scientific perceptions of reality. Causal explanations are avoided.

Grounded theory

Grounded theory (Glaser and Strauss 1967) is used to study social interactions and experiences. It aims to explain processes and develop theory that is grounded in the data through both deductive and inductive reasoning. It does not test existing hypotheses or theories. Grounded theory does not aim to find the truth but instead seeks to develop concepts and theory through the use of empirical methods, which can include focus groups, interviews and questionnaires, for example.

Phenomenological research

Phenomenology is the study of the nature and meanings of phenomena. The aim is to understand and describe the structure of lived experience, or the 'life-world', rather than explain it. Phenomenological research often begins with concrete descriptions of the lived world in a person's own words. These are then analysed, reflected upon and described. Researchers need to put aside their own perceptions about the phenomena under study so that they can approach their work without preconceptions.

Heuristic inquiry

Heuristic inquiry is an adaptation of phenomenological inquiry described above. Instead of putting aside preconceptions, the researcher acknowledges their involvement, to the extent that the lived experience of the researcher becomes one of the main focuses of the research. Heuristic inquiry searches for essential meanings connected with everyday human experiences. Imagination, intuition and self-reflection are important aspects of heuristic inquiry.

Action research

Action research is an interactive inquiry process (between the researcher and participants) that moves forward to solve problems, improve practice or develop strategies, for example. It moves beyond reflective knowledge, using empirical methods to develop well-informed action. Broadly speaking, the group moves through four stages of planning, acting, observing and reflecting, and various research methods can be used within each stage.

Discourse analysis

Discourse analysis is a general term that is used to describe a number of different approaches to studying and analysing the uses of language (e.g. semiotics and narrative analysis). These techniques have been adopted by social constructionists to help them understand social interactions and underlying social structures. More information about discourse analysis is provided in Chapter 18.

Feminist research

Feminist researchers argue that for too long the lives and experiences of women have been ignored or misrepresented. They critique both the research topics and the methods used, especially those that emphasize objective, scientific 'truth'. With its emphasis on participative, qualitative inquiry, feminist research has provided a valuable alternative framework for researchers who have felt uncomfortable with treating people as research 'objects'.

There are different perspectives within the feminist framework. A brief discussion of these helps to illustrate the interconnectedness between methodology and theoretical perspective (see 'Examples of Feminist Perspectives' box, opposite).

Examples of Feminist Perspectives

Feminist empiricism seeks to discover a more objective truth by eliminating such biases as gender, class and race from the research process. Traditional Western scholarship and science is seen to have been developed purely from a white, male, middle-class perspective and research has been conducted from this standpoint, eliminating or belittling the experiences of 'subordinate' groups.

Feminist standpoint research asks whether it is possible to have feminist methods because feminism itself is constantly changing and being redefined (Harding 1991; Griffin 1995). Feminist standpoint research suggests that knowledge is shaped by the social context of the knower, that the perspective of marginalized groups in society is most complete because it reflects the experience of the disadvantaged within the dominant culture (Wuest 1995: 126). As knowledge is constructed from the position of the knower, science is part of the social order and is viewed and produced exclusively by the powerful in society.

Feminist postmodernism suggests that there is no single truth that can be researched and reported, as women's experiences vary according to age, race, class, culture, sexual orientation, education and other variables. Basic concepts of power, knowledge and truth are questioned and acknowledged as ever-shifting realities created through the process of social interaction (Wuest 1995: 126). There are multiple explanations of reality and it is important to look for the basic social process that leads to variation in behaviour within the conditions imposed by the existing structure of society.

Summary

Research methodology is the overall system or framework that is used to guide your research project. Your methodology is influenced by your epistemological standpoint and by your theoretical perspective. Some standpoints emphasize the importance of objective truth, whereas others suggest that there is no such thing and that the only real truth is constructed by the individual. Within each standpoint there is a variety of methodologies that can be chosen to guide your research.

You need to understand both the epistemological and methodological debate as these issues will help you to think more about the knowledge (and theory) that you intend to generate from your research. The next chapter goes on to discuss generating ideas for your project, illustrating how this process is also influenced by your epistemological and methodological standpoint.

3 Generating Ideas

The way that you generate ideas for your research is influenced, in part, by your epistemological and methodological standpoint. Now that you have read Chapters 1 and 2 you should have more of an understanding of the epistemological and methodological debates and can, therefore, move on to generating your ideas further.

This chapter discusses the various ways that you can generate ideas for your research project, helping you to think about your topic, develop your research question and create ideas inductively and/or deductively, depending on your epistemological and methodological standpoint.

Developing Your Topic

Your research topic must be of interest to you (to help maintain motivation) and it must be worthy of your research efforts (relevant, timely, helping to develop new knowledge or building on existing knowledge). It must also be a topic that enables you to carry out research at the right intellectual and academic level.

If you are yet to decide on a topic for your research there are a number of different methods that you can use to generate ideas.

- Brainstorming: using this method you think about an issue and write down any thoughts that come to mind, without judgement or reflection. The goal is to come up with a list that can be returned to, discussed and analysed at a later date. Brainstorming can be a useful way to generate ideas if you are struggling to find a suitable focus for your research.

- Lateral thinking: this involves approaching an issue through an indirect route that does not follow logical ways of thought. This method of thinking is useful if you want to create new ideas, perhaps for a unique research project on a topic that has not been covered before.

- Critical thinking: this involves making judgements about an issue, idea or concept. This type of thinking can be used when trying to understand, evaluate, analyse and develop your own research question. It can also be useful if you want to critique previous research or add to existing knowledge on a particular topic.

- Logical thinking: this way of thinking follows a rational, sequential order. This method is useful for researchers from the objectivist standpoint, who perhaps wish to conduct experimental or survey research, for example.

- Visualization: you can create a picture to help you to think about your research, or you may decide to draw a graph or a diagram that helps you to clarify your thoughts. Visualization can be a useful method to adopt for complex themes or concepts that are difficult to order into a linear sequence, for example.

- Observing: using this method you take note of phenomena or behaviour that, in your opinion, needs further investigation to explain patterns, behaviour or processes. Asking further questions about your observations will help to stimulate your thoughts (see 'Asking Questions to Stimulate Thought' box, below).

■ Experiencing: using this method you encounter phenomena or behaviour that, in your opinion, requires further investigation. Again, asking in-depth questions about your experiences will help to stimulate your thoughts and further develop your research topic (see 'Asking Questions to Stimulate Thought' box, below).

Asking Questions to Stimulate Thought

There are different types of questions that you can ask to stimulate your thoughts and help you to arrive at a suitable topic and/or research question. These include questions of:

purpose

information

interpretation

accuracy

relevance

meaning

They also include questions that:

stimulate reflection

introduce a problem

lead to deep and critical thought

test existing assumptions and/or knowledge

Developing Your Research Question

Your research question is a clear, concise and complex question around which your research is focused. It needs to be specific and defendable. Research questions tend to be easier to generate when much is known about a topic and there are clear and well-developed theoretical frameworks in place. They can be harder to generate in cases where little is known about a subject or where the emphasis is on knowledge discovery or theoretical development.

Your research question can be developed by working through the stages listed below:

1. Choose a topic (see 'Developing Your Topic', above).

2. Undertake some preliminary background research to find out about other research on this topic. Are you able to add to existing knowledge or develop new knowledge on the topic? (Some researchers from the subjectivist and constructionist standpoints might argue that background research should not be undertaken at this stage because it may prevent the researcher from being truly open to new ideas and thoughts.)

3. Who is your audience? If the research is for a postgraduate course or PhD, does the topic provide enough scope to work at the right intellectual level?

4. What is the goal of your research? This could be to build on existing knowledge or encourage change in practice, for example.

5. Start to ask relevant questions and pick the one that is most suitable.

6. Develop this question into your research question (see 'Attributes of a Good Research Question' box, below). Make sure that it is focused and complex (that is, it cannot

be answered with a simple yes or no based on existing knowledge).

7. Reflect, analyse and/or hypothesize. Is your question suitable and workable?

8. Seek advice. Does your supervisor, employer or fellow student(s) think that your research question is suitable, focused, clear, complex and workable?

9. Revise as appropriate.

Attributes of a Good Research Question

The research question should lead to research that extends or adds to existing knowledge.

The question should be well formulated, credible and easy to understand.

Questions that are stated in hypothetical form (within the objectivist stance, for example) will need to lead to a research design and analysis that holds scientific credibility.

The research question should allow for more than one outcome and the possibility that the working hypothesis (if relevant) can be refuted.

The research question should allow for variability and different results under a variety of conditions.

The research question should allow for adaptation and change (within the constructionist standpoint, for example).

The research question must be workable and allow for the collection of the required data over time and within budget.

Changing your research question

In most cases your research question, once developed and deemed suitable, will remain the same throughout your research, helping to guide you through the research and writing process. However, if your methodology has been developed from within the constructionist or subjectivist standpoints, it may be necessary to alter the research question as the research progresses. This may be because the underlying premise cannot be supported or emerging data suggest that the initial question is not salient in the context studied, for example.

Tip If you need to change your research question you must re-analyse your data in light of the new question, taking great care not to develop a new question that merely fits with an emerging hypothesis.

Generating Ideas Inductively

From a subjectivist and constructionist standpoint a researcher does not identify with an objective truth that can be studied. Instead, the researcher's task is to describe, explain and/or understand a particular group, culture, society, structure or process before developing and/or testing theory.

This type of research design in the initial stages, therefore, is inductive. It is emergent, flexible and dynamic. The ideas that are generated in the early stages of the work can have a substantial influence on later stages, but it is also important to allow for adaptation, development and change as the project progresses. However, some methodologies are more flexible than others when allowing for this type of change, so you need to consider these methodological issues when generating your topic and research question.

It is also important to note that certain methodologies provide a framework that is non-linear and non-sequential (data collection and analysis proceed simultaneously). In some cases it may be unclear at the start of your project where your research will take you as it progresses. Again, you will need to bear in mind these issues when developing your research topic and generating your research question. Both will need to be flexible enough to allow for this type of change.

Generating Ideas Deductively

From an objectivist point of view objects exist to be studied, independent of consciousness. As such, researchers from this standpoint employ deductive techniques, drawing heavily on existing and substantive prior knowledge to conceptualize specific situations. Your research framework will enable you to make predictions and provide explanations about the behaviour of particular people and groups.

Researchers approaching their work from this standpoint often find it much easier to generate research topics and questions at the beginning of their project as these are based on existing knowledge and/or observations. Also, the research project will follow a logical, sequential order. While flexibility and adaptability are less important, you will need to demonstrate that you can follow procedures, present the required evidence and pay close attention to issues of validity and reliability. You will need to bear these issues in mind when developing your topic and generating your research question.

Mixed approaches

For some projects it might be appropriate to use a mixture of deductive and inductive techniques for generating ideas. For example, while the main topic of the research might suggest an inductive process in the early stages, the interaction between conceptual and empirical elements as the project develops may require a more deductive process. Again, it is important to think about these methodological issues when developing your topic and generating your research question so that you can allow for this type of flexibility, if required.

Summary

As an advanced researcher it is important to spend time developing your topic and research question. There are various methods that you can use to help you to do this, including brainstorming, lateral thinking and visualization. You need to ensure that your topic will enable you to conduct research at the right intellectual level, and that your research question is clear, concise and workable. Your epistemological and methodological position will have a bearing on the ideas and questions that you generate for your project.

Once you have developed a suitable topic and research question it is important to be able to justify your research (this will also help you to tighten your topic, research question and methodological framework). These issues are discussed in the next chapter.

4 Justifying Your Research

It is important to be able to justify your research in terms of topic, research question and methodology early in the planning stage. This will help you to understand the relevance, timeliness, importance and uniqueness of your project and alert you to any potential problems early in your work. It is also important because it will help you to think more about justifying your research when you come to write your thesis and undertake your viva (if relevant).

This chapter provides advice about justifying your topic, justifying your research question and defending your methodology. If you are unable to justify your research early in the planning process you may need to think again about the focus of your work, redefine your project and/or rework your research question (see Chapter 3).

Justifying Your Topic

Working through a process of topic justification will help you to decide whether your proposed project is viable, workable, exciting, important and worth your time and effort. Exercise 2 will help you to do this.

When you justify your topic it is also important to consider how you decided on the topic: is it a valid, reliable and justifiable reason for undertaking the research? For example, if the idea for the research developed from personal experience, you need to reflect on this experience, relate it to the existing literature and point out how your research will add to existing knowledge.

Exercise 2: Asking Questions about Your Topic

When justifying your topic, work through the following questions (remember to keep comprehensive notes as you work through this process as they will provide valuable information to include in your thesis/report and viva):

What is exciting about the topic?

Why is research on this topic needed?

How can you add to existing knowledge or develop new knowledge on this topic?

What is original about this topic? (Or perhaps it is the approach to the topic that is original: see 'Justifying Your Research Question', below.)

What is the likelihood of success in your research, when compared with other work in this field and in its own right?

Why is research on this topic useful and worthwhile?

What is the expected impact of your research on this topic?

Justifying Your Research Question

As we have seen in Chapter 3, your research question guides you through the research and writing process. Your research project will succeed only if you have asked the right question. It is important, therefore, to be able to justify and defend your question at the start of your project. Exercise 3 will help you to do this.

> **Exercise 3: Analysing Your Research Question**
>
> Chapter 3 provides a list of the attributes of a good research question. Critically analyse your research question with reference to this list. Take some time to do this: it is essential that your research question is as good as it can be and that you are able to justify and defend your question. If you have any doubts, seek advice from your supervisor or a work colleague.

Defending Your Methodology

Methodological defence is an extremely important part of your research, especially for those who choose a more innovative, less well-known methodology. Chapter 2 highlights important issues concerning the methodological debate, and you should work through these before making your choice.

Once you have chosen a suitable methodology you must be able to defend your choice. Exercise 4 will help you to do this. By working through this exercise you will be able to make sure that your methodological choice fits with your theoretical perspective and epistemological standpoint, and that your methodology is the most suitable framework for your chosen topic and research question. Again, keep all notes as this will provide important information for your thesis and viva.

Exercise 4: Asking Methodological Questions

Work through the following questions. Once you have done this ask a fellow student, work colleague or supervisor to listen to your defence. Ask for their feedback and alter your defence, or refine your methodology, accordingly.

Why have you chosen your methodology?

Why is your chosen methodology the most appropriate for your topic?

How does your methodology help you to work towards answering your research question?

What other methodologies could have been chosen and why were they rejected?

How does your chosen methodology fit with your epistemological standpoint and theoretical perspective?

Is it possible to refine, combine or alter your methodology (if required) yet still retain a coherent epistemological position?

Tip Take care to avoid methodological fundamentalism when defending your methodology. This implies that your methodology is the one true approach and that all other methodologies are inferior and/or flawed. Be prepared to critique your methodology and change/adapt/combine if necessary.

Summary

As a researcher working on an advanced project it is vital that you are able to justify your research topic, your research question and your methodology. You must do this at the beginning of your project because it will help you to clarify your thoughts and discover problems that can be rectified quickly, before your research project is under way. All arguments in defence of your project at this stage will be useful when you come to write your thesis and undertake your viva on completion (if relevant).

Once you have justified and defended your research project successfully you can go on to think about and list your aims and objectives. These issues are discussed in the following chapter.

5 Developing Aims and Objectives

Now that you have become more familiar with the epistemological and methodological debates, and once you are sufficiently happy with, and can justify, your research question and topic, you can begin to develop your aims and objectives. Developing clear aims and objectives will ensure that there is no confusion over your research topic, methodology and methods. Once developed, they will help to guide you through each stage of your project and help you to answer your research question on completion of your work.

This chapter offers advice about developing well-designed aims and objectives, illustrating how to avoid pitfalls and demonstrating how your aims and objectives are important throughout the research process.

Defining Aims and Objectives

The aim is the overall driving force of your research. It is a simple and broad statement of intent that describes exactly what you want to achieve from your research. It should emphasize what is to be accomplished and address the outcomes of your project.

It is possible to have more than one aim. However, you will find it useful to develop just one clear and succinct aim as it forces you to focus on what, exactly, you want from your research. Alternatively, it is possible to produce one main aim and one or two subsidiary aims, if this is better suited to your project.

The objectives are the means by which you intend to achieve the aims. They are detailed and more specific statements that describe specifically how you are going to address your research question. Between five and ten objectives is usually a good number, but this can be flexible, depending on the type of research. The main point is to make sure that your objectives show how you intend to meet your aim(s).

Tip If you are a postgraduate student, speak to your supervisor before developing your aims and objectives. This is because some courses/departments require aims and objectives to be produced in a specific format.

Producing Aims and Objectives

Your research question (see Chapter 3) will help you to produce your aims and objectives. You should also bear in mind the following:

- Produce aims and objectives that are clear, succinct and unambiguous, taking care to define any technical terms used.

- Be concise and brief.

- Make sure that your objectives relate to your aim(s).

- Provide an indication of how your inquiry will proceed; this is not a specific statement of methods, but will give an indication through the terms used, for example 'identify', 'describe', 'explain', 'observe', etc. This will also give an indication of your epistemological and methodological preferences (see 'Example: Aims and Objectives for a PhD Thesis', below).

- Produce aims and objectives that support your methodology (for example, you should only mention the intention to generalize when this is your methodological goal).

- Provide an indication of the long-term outcome, such as 'produce an analysis' and 'develop associated theory' (see 'Example: Aims and Objectives for a PhD Thesis', below).

- Produce aims and objectives that are realistic in terms of what you can achieve during your research (available resources, time, access to participants, for example).

- Make sure that each objective is distinct and does not merely repeat another using different terms.

- Take care not to produce a list of issues that are merely related to your research topic and/or methods.

Example: Aims and Objectives for a PhD Thesis (Adult Education)

Aim

To identify, describe and produce an analysis of the interacting factors that influence the learning choices of adult returners, and to develop associated theory.

Objectives

The research seeks to determine:

1. The nature, extent and effect of psychological influences on choices, including a desire to achieve personal goals or meet individual needs.

2. The nature, extent and effect of sociological influences on choices, including background, personal and social expectations, previous educational experience and social role.

3. The nature and influence of individual perceptions of courses, institutions and subjects, and how these relate to self-perception and concept of self.

4. The influence on choice of a number of variables such as age, gender, ethnicity and social class.

5. The role and possible influence of significant others on choice, such as advice and guidance workers, peers, relatives and employers.

6. The nature and extent of possible influences on choice of available provision, institutional advertising and marketing.

7. The nature and extent of possible influences on choice of mode of study, teaching methods and type of course.

8. How and to what extent influencing factors change as adults re-enter and progress through their chosen route.

Using Aims and Objectives

Aims and objectives should be referred to throughout the research process to ensure that your research remains on track. This is of particular importance during the design of your methods, the data collection and the data analysis stages. For example, if you intend to design a questionnaire for a large survey, each component or each question must be linked back to your aims and objectives. This will stop you asking irrelevant questions and will help to ensure that your questionnaire produces the type of information required to answer your research question.

When you come to the conclusion of your project you will need to assess whether you have met your aims and objectives. If you have not met them, analyse why and state this in your thesis/report. There could be a number of reasons, such as variables that could not be considered during the planning stages, or new insights that are essential to your research question but had not been identified in your aims and objectives. A thorough critical analysis can help to improve your thesis or report, so don't think that you have failed if you have not been able to meet all your aims and objectives.

Tip   Make sure that your aims and objectives give a clear indication of the four 'w's of your research (who, why, when, where), and also an indication of how your research will proceed. These should not be stated explicitly, but should be implicit within your aims and objectives.

Summary

Aims and objectives are developed from your research question and help to provide a focus and guide for your project. The aim is a simple and broad statement of intent and the objectives are the means by which you intend to achieve the aim. All statements should be clear, concise and unambiguous, with all terms explained. Your aims and objectives should be referred to throughout the research process as this will help you to make sure that your research remains on track.

Once you have developed a list of aims and objectives you can think about planning your project. The next section of this book goes on to look at these planning issues, beginning with advice about costing your project.

STAGE 2

PLANNING YOUR PROJECT

6 Costing Your Project

When you begin to plan your research project you need to think about the cost. This will help you to work out whether your project is feasible and viable, and whether you will be able to complete the work within budget. Costing your project is of particular importance if you intend to apply for research funding or are expecting an employer to pay for the research (see Chapter 7).

All important costs must be included to ensure that your research is of the highest quality. Financial concerns and problems can impinge on the effectiveness of your research. If you are able to cost your project well from the outset and obtain the right amount of money, you can concentrate on your research rather than worry about your budget. This chapter offers advice about how to do this.

Working Out Costs

Some funding organizations request that costs are split into direct and indirect costs. Direct costs include research staff, equipment, travel and subsistence. Indirect costs (often referred to as facilities and administrative costs) include associated staff (e.g. clerical and technical), accommodation and services. Consider the following points when working out your costs:

■ If you are applying for external funding and you work in a university, seek advice from your university research office as members of staff will be able to offer advice about Full Economic Costing (see Chapter 7). Also, you must make sure that you read and understand the guidelines produced by the funding organization.

■ If you are a research student, seek advice from your supervisor. You may need to find out what funds and resources are available for your use, especially if you need additional hardware or software that is not already available.

■ Find out whether there is a cap on the budget for your research. If there is, this could have a considerable influence on your research methods and the amount of travel you can undertake (for conferences and data collection, for example).

■ Find out whether there are any expenses that will not be paid. For example, some funding organizations will not pay for certain types of travel or will specify that you have to use the cheapest means possible if you wish to claim your expenses. Also, most will not pay for alcohol or entertainment.

■ Many researchers (especially postgraduate students) are expected to meet most small costs themselves. This is often covered within studentships or grants. However, if you are struggling financially and cannot meet these costs, discuss the issue with your supervisor and/or students' union.

Tip Researchers who are new to the costing process often underestimate the amount of staff time required to undertake a task (researcher and associated staff time). In these cases it is better to overestimate, rather than underestimate.

Preparing a Research Budget

Your research budget is a financial proposal that reflects your research project and, as such, should mirror your project description. It is a detailed statement that outlines the costs of the work involved.

The type, content and style of your budget statement depend on the type of funding you require for your project. For example, if you intend to apply for a grant from an external funding organization, in most cases, you will need to produce a comprehensive budget that follows a set format (see Chapter 7). However, if you are a research student you may only need to provide a general guide to costs and an indication of the resources that will be required for your research. This will help you to work out the feasibility of your project within your budget and timescale.

Budget preparation questions

When preparing your budget you need to answer the following questions (remember that these may need to be split into direct and indirect costs):

- Do you need to purchase anything for your research? This could include computing hardware or software, materials such as stationery and stamps, or the services of others, such as administration or data-input services.

- Are there any salaries to be paid as part of your research? This can include salaries of the researcher and associated staff, for example (see Chapter 7).

- Are there any communications and marketing costs, such as telephone calls, advertisements to attract participants or the use of outside consultants? Your university/employer communications and/or marketing office will be able to provide information and advice on marketing issues.

- Do you have to budget for rooms and accommodation? For example, if you are to run focus groups do you need to hire a room and, if so, how much does it cost? (The room must be accessible physically and mentally to participants: see Chapter 12.)

- Will there be any travel costs? This could include travel to interviews or focus groups, or travel to conferences to present a paper, for example.

- Are there any publication costs, such as printing and binding of your thesis, printing of questionnaires or dissemination of papers/reports or briefings (including open access publishing costs: see Chapter 25)?

Sourcing Figures for Your Budget

Getting your figures right shows that you are competent and organized, and that you understand the true costs of your research, which is of particular importance when applying for funding. There are various ways to source figures for your budget:

- university or employer salary scales and benefits database;
- your university research office;
- your estates management department;
- your human resources department;
- your communications/marketing office;
- quotations from internal departments, such as your university/employer printing and binding service;

- quotations from vendors (some funding organizations will ask that you obtain more than one quotation);
- tenders or contracts from outside individuals/organizations;
- your supervisor and department administration office.

Justifying Your Budget

When preparing your budget you must be able to justify all the costs. Both internal and external funding organizations will want to see value for money and will not provide funds that are inappropriate or cannot be justified in relation to the proposed research (see Chapter 7). Indeed, some funding organizations have a separate section on the application form for budget justification.

You will need to highlight, explain and provide a rationale for each section of your budget. Also, you will need to make it clear that any request for funds is appropriate and consistent with your university, employer and/or the funding organization policies. Even if you are not applying for funding, it is useful to complete this justification process as it enables you to work through and check your budget in line with your project description.

Tip All costs must be realistic, reasonable, justifiable, allowable and allocatable (necessary for the success of the project). All figures should be presented clearly and added up correctly (ask a competent person to check them, if in doubt).

Summary

Costing your research project is an important part of the planning process, especially if you intend to apply for external funding. Working through the costs and preparing a budget enables you to break down each part of your research and work out whether your project is viable in terms of budget and resources. It is important to make sure that you have enough money to complete the work and that all costs can be justified.

If you are intending to apply for internal or external funding for your research, you will need to work out your costs and produce your budget in a specific way, following the guidelines produced by the funding organization. These issues are discussed in the next chapter.

7 Obtaining Funding

Now that you have worked out the cost of your project you will need to obtain funding. This could be from your university, from an external funding organization (a charity or research funding council, for example) or from your employer. All funding organizations will only meet acceptable costs and all will want to see value for money, in terms of strategic importance and research impact.

This chapter offers advice about obtaining funding from both external and internal sources, knowing how to make a successful application and avoiding problems with funding applications. At the end of the book, the 'References, Further Reading and Resources' section for this chapter includes websites that contain searchable databases of funding sources.

Obtaining External Funding

If you intend to attract external funding for your project, contact your university research office or employer finance office for information. Members of staff will be able to offer advice about sources of funding, the application process and, for university researchers, information about Full Economic Costing (see 'Knowing About Full Economic Costing', p. 49).

Sources of external funding

Public funds

Public funds can be obtained from Research Councils, the National Health Service, the European Commission and government departments, for example (see 'Useful Websites' under 'References, Further Reading and Resources' for this chapter at the end of the book). Most of these organizations have well-defined rules, procedures and guidelines for costing projects and preparing proposals, so you must find out about these before you begin your application. This will enable you to check that your project is relevant and that it will be considered for funding.

Private funds

Private funds are available through charities, trusts, industry and wealthy individuals, for example. Larger private funders have well-defined procedures and application processes, so you must read all guidelines before making an application. Smaller trusts and charities might not have set procedures and may only provide funds for specific purposes such as travel or staff costs.

If possible, contact the funders direct so that you can find out whether your project has a chance of being funded before you prepare your proposal.

Tip   When collaborating with other organizations/universities there might be ownership issues over equipment that was bought using funds provided for the project. You need to address these issues when you prepare your proposal. This should prevent problems occurring on completion of the research.

Obtaining Internal Funding

Internal funds are available from your employer, university, department, school and/or faculty. The amount and type of funding varies enormously, so you will need to discuss internal funding with your employer, supervisor or the university research office to find out how to proceed.

You will need to demonstrate how your research fits in with the work and profile of your department/faculty or how it is relevant to the work of your organization. You should also be able to demonstrate the relevance of your supervisor's work to your own proposed research, if appropriate. If you are a postgraduate student who has already gone through this process during the application stage you should find this a simple matter.

Tip Good research will bring external recognition and can help universities and organizations to attract additional funding. This can help you to provide a justification for your research. However, you must make sure that your research will not use money and resources that your department or employer cannot afford, would find hard to meet or cannot sustain.

Knowing About Full Economic Costing

In September 2005 the UK government introduced Full Economic Costing (fEC). This is a method used by higher education institutions across the UK to calculate the cost of research projects, and takes account of all direct costs and associated indirect and estates costs. The abbreviation fEC is used rather than FEC because the latter is recognized as referring to Further Education Colleges.

The way that fEC is applied can vary, depending on the funder and the university. Your research office will provide further guidance about fEC and help you to complete the application process.

Preparing a Funding Proposal

Funders have distinct thematic research priorities that inform their funding decisions. Therefore, when preparing a funding proposal you must make sure that you are applying to the most appropriate organization and that you have the most up-to-date guidelines. Consider the following points when preparing your proposal:

- Find out whether you need to follow a set format for costing and, if so, make sure you understand and follow this format. Obtain and use all the relevant forms. Failure to do this can lead to immediate rejection.

- Find out what will and will not be funded. For example, some funders will not allow for administrative support and others will not allow permanent staff time to be charged.

- Seek advice about salary scales and increments.

- When seeking funds for equipment you will need to justify its use. If you need to include quotations from suppliers, allow time to do this. Depreciation costs may need to be included.

- Your university or organization may have rules about tendering, procurement and using certain suppliers. Find out whether this is the case before developing your proposal.

- Although most funders won't pay for stationery, you may be able to make a claim if it is part of your research (a large-scale postal survey, for example).

- Include IT supplies if your research involves a large amount of data storage and use of software, for example.

▪ Remember to include all travel and subsistence costs such as fares and accommodation at conferences.

▪ Find out the preferred method for invoicing and payment procedures so that you can keep all records correctly.

▪ Ask an experienced person or your employer to check your application form. Members of staff in your university research office will be happy to do this. Make sure that your figures add up. Ask someone to check them for you (your supervisor, employer or staff within the research office).

▪ Obtain all the necessary signatures. This will include all applicants, your head of department (or employer) and any other collaborators.

▪ Submit your application for review and authorization by your research office or your employer (if relevant) at least five days before the deadline. If you are only asking for a small sum of money with no associated staff costs you might not have to submit for authorization.

Tip Most funding organizations will not increase their offer of funding, so you must make sure that you cover all costs in your proposal.

Making Successful Funding Applications

To be successful in obtaining funding for your research you must choose the best and most relevant source for your funds. You must be able to justify the costs (see Chapter 6) and justify your research (see Chapter 4). The advantages and disadvantages of the project must be weighed carefully and you will need to demonstrate the strategic importance and impact of your research. Universities, employers and external funders will only meet acceptable costs and the funds requested must be appropriate for the project. Also, the funders will want to see value for money.

Pay close attention to detail. Most funders will reject applications that have not correctly addressed issues such as page length, font size and supporting evidence (such as CVs, quotations, justification of resources, impact statements and letters of collaboration). Funding organizations, in most cases, will not allow you to resubmit this information.

You may find it useful to read previous successful bids and seek advice from colleagues with experience. If you are in doubt about application procedures or rules, seek advice from the relevant funding organization or from your university research office.

Tip   Consider the time involved in preparing a funding bid and think about the likelihood of success. Bids for funding can take a long time and if you are unsuccessful you will need to allocate time for amendments/rewriting or the development of a new bid.

Summary

There is a variety of funding organizations that provide money for academic research, including public funders, private funders and internal funders. Your research must be matched to the appropriate funder and you must be able to justify your research and the costs involved. It is also important to demonstrate the strategic importance and impact of your research.

Once you have worked out the cost of your project and achieved success in obtaining funding for your work, you can go on to collect background information. These issues are discussed in the following chapter.

8 Collecting Background Information

Collecting background information will help you to get a broad overview of your topic, introduce you to key ideas and current thinking, help you to identify gaps in existing knowledge and enable you to refine and develop your research proposal (see Chapter 11). It will also enable you to develop your research methodology further (see Chapter 2).

This chapter guides you through the process, illustrating how collecting background information is influenced and informed by your epistemological standpoint, theoretical perspective and chosen research methodology. It goes on to provide practical advice about collecting and critically analysing background information.

Locating Your Standpoint and Collecting Information

The methods that you use to collect background information for your research will be influenced by your epistemological and methodological standpoint and by theoretical perspective (see Chapters 1 and 2).

Objectivist standpoint

If you locate yourself within the objectivist standpoint (that objective knowledge can be obtained through deductive reasoning and the truth found through replicable observation), background information is readily available in the form of research papers, journal articles, books and so on (unless, of course, you have chosen a truly unique topic).

You can analyse and critique previous work and develop your own research question and/or hypotheses based on this previous work. You can also refer to the background literature throughout your project if it helps you to develop your ideas and theory (see Chapter 21).

Subjectivist standpoint

If you locate yourself within the subjectivist standpoint (that there is no underlying truth and that reality is only what we perceive it to be), background information is approached in a very different way, if, indeed, it is approached at all.

Since researchers from this standpoint are sceptical of claims to objectivity and suspicious of established intellectual categories, previous research may hold little relevance in terms of conclusions. However, the meanings of the texts created by researchers can hold much greater significance for subjectivists. Therefore, any background reading that is undertaken may have more to do with methodology and meanings than with conclusions and established theory.

Constructionist standpoint

If you locate yourself within the constructionist standpoint (that knowledge is constructed by scientists and not discovered from the world), you may be open to a variety of sources of background information, such as previous experience, obser-vation, books, journals and research papers. This will depend on your theoretical perspective and methodological preference.

Those interested in grounded theory, for example, might decide not to undertake a literature review at the beginning of the project, but instead refer to the literature throughout the data collection process to help explain emerging themes and concepts. On the other hand, a researcher involved in action research might read all they can about their particular research topic before they begin their research. This will enable them to become familiar with current thinking, which can then be modified, improved and expanded upon as their action research project progresses.

Tip   Use referencing software to keep a record of any background information you use for your research, even in the very early stages. If you are organized from the start you will be able to find information easily at later stages of your work and you will be able to organize and manage your references as your work progresses. Popular software includes EndNote (http://endnote.com), Zotero (www.zotero.org) and Citeulike (www.citeulike.org).

Finding Background Information

If you are interested in finding background information at the start of your project and as it progresses, there are various sources that you can use, depending on your epistemological, theoretical and methodological preferences (see Chapters 1 and 2).

Primary sources

Primary sources are first-hand narratives, original documents/ objects or factual (not interpretative) accounts that were written or made during or close to the event or period of time. Primary sources that you can use for your background research include:

- historical records/texts;
- government records;
- company/organization records;
- personal documents (diaries, etc.);
- recorded or transcribed speeches or interviews;
- statistical data;
- works of literature;
- works of art;
- film/video;
- published results of laboratory experiments;
- published results of clinical trials;
- published results of research studies;
- conference and seminar proceedings.

Secondary sources

Secondary sources interpret, analyse and critique primary sources. They can provide a second-hand version of events or an interpretation of first-hand accounts, for example. Secondary sources that you can use for your background research include:

- scientific debates;
- analyses of clinical trials;

- analyses/interpretations/critiques of previous research;
- book and article reviews;
- biographies;
- critiques of literary works;
- critiques of art;
- analyses of historical events.

Online Sources of Background Information

Copac (http://copac.ac.uk) enables you to access rare and unique research material by bringing together the catalogues of over seventy major UK and Irish libraries, including the British Library, the National Library of Scotland and the National Library of Wales. Copac does not hold any of the materials so you will need to arrange an inter-library loan with your local or university library.

Directory of Open Access Journals (www.doaj.org) offers free online access to high-quality academic papers, and provides useful quick and advanced search facilities to help you find relevant articles (see Chapter 25).

Google Scholar (http://scholar.google.com) enables you to search scholarly literature such as books, articles, theses and abstracts from academic publishers, professional societies, online repositories, universities and other websites. You can use the 'settings' menu to access the 'library links' to locate documents in university libraries. Links to other documents located on the web are also available. However, many papers will require a subscription to read them, so you may need to contact your university library for more information and to access papers.

Google Books (http://books.google.com) enables you to search for books that are out of copyright (or where the publisher has given permission for them to be published by Google). In some cases you will be able to see a preview of the book and in other cases you will be able to read the entire text (you can download a PDF if the book is in the public domain). You can also use the service to buy or borrow books.

Evaluating Background Information

When evaluating background information, you should ask the following questions:

Author's credentials:

- Who is the author?
- What else has the author written?
- What is their educational background and what qualifications are held?
- What position does the author hold and where?

Date of publication:

- When was the article published (or what is the date of copyright)?
- How up-to-date is the material, given your knowledge of the topic?
- Have the ideas been developed and moved on since this material was published?

Edition or revision:

- Is this the latest edition of the work?
- Are recent revisions made clear?

Publisher:

- Who is the publisher and are they considered reliable/scholarly?
- What reason does the publisher have for making the work available?

Type of publication:

- Is the journal peer-reviewed or refereed?
- Is the article/book correctly referenced, with all sources cited (footnotes, bibliographies and references)?

Intended audience:

- Is the material aimed at a generalist or specialist audience?
- Is it at the right level for your requirements?
- Is there other material available that would be more appropriate?

Coverage:

- Is the material a primary or secondary source (see 'Primary sources' and 'Secondary sources', above)?
- Does the material update other sources or add to existing information?
- How much of your topic is covered by the material?

Reasoning:

- Does the article discuss statistics, facts, opinions, arguments or propaganda (see Chapter 20)?
- Are arguments well backed up by evidence?
- Are statistics valid and reliable (see Chapter 19)?

Methods:

- What methods were used to generate the data presented?
- Are the methods well described and sound?

Writing style:

- Is the article easy to understand?
- Are all technical terms explained?

Reviews:

- Can you find any third-party reviews?
- Are reviews positive or negative?
- Can you find any citations?

Follow-up:

- Can you find any other material that supports the work?
- Can you find any other material that opposes the work?

For more information about critiquing and reviewing quantitative and qualitative research papers and reports, see Chapter 20.

Tip When evaluating background information, be aware of making subjective judgements that are influenced by personal bias. This is an inclination or preference that influences your judgement, often in a subtle way that may be difficult to detect. See Chapter 20 for more information about recognizing the different types of bias.

Summary

When collecting background information it is important to consider your epistemological and methodological standpoint, and the theoretical perspective that underpins your research, as this will have an influence on the type, amount and timing of what you collect. All material must be analysed critically. This is especially so when obtaining information from sources that have not gone through a process of peer review.

In addition to collecting background information about your .topic, you will also need to read more about your intended methodology as this helps to inform your choice of research methods. More information about methodology is provided in Chapter 2 and more information about research methods is provided in the following chapter.

9 Choosing Research Methods

It is not possible to answer your research question or meet your aims and objectives without a careful choice of research methods. These are the tools that you will use to gather and analyse your data and can include sampling techniques, questionnaires, interviews, focus groups, case studies, experiments, trials, qualitative data analysis techniques and quantitative data analysis techniques.

This chapter helps you to think more about your research methods, illustrating how your choice of methods evolves from your epistemological standpoint, theoretical perspective and methodological position.

Relating Methods to Epistemology, Theoretical Perspective and Methodology

In Chapter 2 we saw how Crotty (1998) identifies three epistemological positions and discusses these in terms of their relationship to theoretical perspective and methodology. He then goes on to discuss this further, illustrating how these relationships have an influence on the choice of research methods (see Fig. 3).

However, it is important to note that, even though your research method choices are influenced by epistemology, theoretical perspective and methodology, these choices are not necessarily constrained by them. For example, although researchers may use focus groups to gather feedback and opinions on a certain product (in market research: objectivist standpoint), they can also be used to tighten and clarify emerging theory (in a grounded theory study, for example: constructionist).

Fig. 3: The Influence of Epistemology, Theoretical Perspective and Methodology on Research Methods (Source: adapted from Crotty 1998)

Objectivism → positivism, post-positivism → experimental research, survey research → quantitative questionnaires, structured interviews, experiments, sampling techniques, statistical analysis, content analysis

Subjectivism → postmodernism, structuralism, post-structuralism → discourse theory, deconstruction → literary analysis, semiotics, dialectical analysis, textual analysis

Constructionism → interpretivism (symbolic interactionism, phenomenology, hermeneutics), critical inquiry, feminism → ethnography, grounded theory, phenomenological research, heuristic inquiry, action research, discourse analysis, feminist research → life histories, case studies, focus groups, scenario research, participant observation, thematic analysis

Exercise 5: Connecting Methods, Methodology and Epistemology

Refer back to the epistemological and methodological debates (see Chapters 1 and 2) and make sure that you have not, unthinkingly, located yourself within an inappropriate position for your research topic. Check that you can work through the following: epistemological standpoint → theoretical perspective → methodological position → research methods. Determine whether your standpoint enables a multiple or mixed approach and, if so, consider research methods that are suitable within this approach (see 'Using Multiple or Mixed Approaches' below).

Using Multiple or Mixed Approaches

We have seen above that the epistemological and methodological standpoint has an influence on methods but does not, necessarily, constrain choices. As we have seen in Chapter 2, you can use a multiple or mixed approach for your research. This requires a flexible position that enables you to move between the different standpoints. For example, you may take the objectivist view that human beings are born into a society that already exists and can be studied, but you may also consider the constructionist view that structures evolve and change through human interaction.

Multiple and mixed approaches enable you to take these different views into account and choose your research methods accordingly. For example, you may use a questionnaire to generate statistics about a phenomenon that is observable, but then run some focus groups to help explain some unexpected findings (see Chapters 12 and 14). Or perhaps you decide to gather data using semi-structured interviews (within a qualitative framework), but then choose to analyse the transcripts using content analysis, counting the number of keyword occurrences (within a quantitative framework), for example (see Chapters 13 and 18).

Tip   If you choose to use a multiple or mixed approach, you must take into account the understanding of your audience: granting bodies, examiners and stakeholders may approach the work with their own biases and methodological/method preferences. You will need to become very familiar with the mix of methodologies/methods and persuade others that this approach is the best and most appropriate for your research.

Choosing the Most Appropriate Methods

When choosing your research methods, consider the following points:

- Conduct a thorough review of the methodological and methods literature. Read Stages 3 and 4 of this book for in-depth information about particular types of research method. Become familiar with the options that are available. Critically analyse other research that has used the methods so that you can understand particular strengths and weaknesses.

- Decide whether your research is exploratory, descriptive or causal (or a combination of these), and match your methods accordingly.

- Make sure that the purpose of your research matches the methods that you choose. For example, if you choose to generate theory by using a grounded theory methodology, you need to use research methods that will help you to do this, such as interviews, focus groups and a simultaneous literature review (to provide insight into emerging concepts). If your purpose is to test existing theory you can use methods such as statistical modelling or postal questionnaires, for example.

- Choose methods that you are comfortable with, interested in and that are ethically sound (see Chapter 27).

- Make sure that you choose methods that are practicable in terms of time, resources and feasibility.

Piloting your methods

Once you have made your choice, always pilot (test) data-collection instruments to ensure that they are suitable, feasible and workable, and that they are able to generate the type of data that will help to answer your research question and meet your aims and objectives. Modify and retest accordingly.

Tip Choose and use your methods with care: validity stems from the appropriateness of methods and the thoroughness and effectiveness with which they have been applied. Don't be tempted to skip the piloting stage.

Summary

Research methods are the tools that you use to carry out your research. When choosing your research methods you need to consider your epistemological standpoint, theoretical perspective and methodological position. If your standpoint is flexible it is possible to choose mixed or multiple methods for your research. When making your choices you must ensure that your methods match the purpose of your research and that they are ethically sound. All methods must be tested thoroughly.

An important research method that you need to think about at this stage of your work is your sampling method. This is of vital importance for those approaching their work from an objectivist standpoint, but is also important for those approaching their work from a constructionist standpoint. Sampling techniques are discussed in the following chapter.

10 Understanding Sampling Techniques

In social research a sample is a set of individuals, groups or items selected from the research population for the purpose of analysis or hypothesis testing. Sampling techniques are used in cases where it is not possible to analyse the whole population (a census). The type of sampling technique that you use, and the assumptions associated with its use, depend on your epistemological and methodological standpoint and on theoretical perspective.

This chapter discusses the various types of sampling technique, provides advice about sample size and illustrates how to avoid making mistakes when choosing and designing your sample.

Knowing About Different Sampling Techniques

There are two main types of sample: probability samples and non-probability samples. There are several different sampling methods within these two categories, as described below.

Probability samples

In probability samples, all people within the study population have a specifiable chance of being selected. These types of sample are used if the researcher wishes to explain, predict or generalize to the whole research population. Since the sample serves as a model for the whole research population, it must be an accurate representation of this population.

Simple random sample

A simple random sample gives each member of the population an equal and known chance of being chosen. Using this procedure a number is assigned to each element/individual in the study population. Random numbers are then generated (using various methods such as calculators, spreadsheets, printed tables of random numbers, for example) to select the required sample. This method requires an accurate list of the study population and is ideal for generating statistics. Problems arise if it is difficult or impossible to identify every member of the population.

Cluster sample

Cluster samples are used when it is impossible or impractical to compile an exhaustive list of all elements within the study population. Instead, the elements are grouped into subpopulations (already existing or created by the researcher) and then elements from each subpopulation are chosen using a simple random sample (described above) or a systematic sample (described below). A problem with this method is an over-represented or under-represented cluster in terms of certain characteristics. This can skew the results of the study.

Systematic sample (or quasi-random sample)

Systematic sampling is a statistical method involving the selection of elements from an ordered study population. A starting point is chosen at random with each subsequent selection made at regular intervals. A problem with this method is that it depends on how the list has been organized (alphabetically, for example).

Stratified random sample

Stratified random sampling is a method of sampling that involves the division of a study population into smaller groups known as strata. These groups may differ in behaviour or in the attribute under study (for example, parents and non-parents). Once the different groups have been identified, members can be selected using a simple random sample or a systematic sample, for example. Problems can arise in the identification of appropriate strata and in analysing results.

Non-probability samples

Non-probability samples (also referred to as purposive samples) are used if description rather than generalization is the goal. In this type of sample it is not possible to specify the possibility of one person being included in the sample. Instead, the sample is selected on the basis of knowledge of the research problem.

Quota sample

Using this technique the sample is selected according to a quota system based on such factors as age, sex and social class. It is a popular method for market researchers. In quota sampling, the researcher aims to represent the major characteristics of the population by sampling a proportional amount of each. Convenience or judgement sampling is used to select the required number of subjects from each category. The proportions in each category must be accurate and care must be taken not to introduce researcher bias (choosing specific people within each category based on their appearance, for example).

Snowball sample

Snowball sampling relies on referrals from initial subjects to generate additional subjects (for example, one interviewee will give the researcher details of another person to be interviewed, and so on). This method is used when it is difficult for subjects to be found, when the study population is small and when description or understanding, rather than generalization, is the goal. Bias can be introduced because the sample does not represent a good section of the population.

Theoretical sampling

Using this method the emerging theory helps the researcher to choose the sample. Within this sampling procedure, the researcher might choose to sample *extreme cases* that help to explain an emerging theme, or might choose *heterogeneous samples* where there is a deliberate strategy to select people who are alike in some relevant detail, for example. Again, the researcher has to be aware of, and note down, sampling bias.

Convenience sample

Convenience sampling (where subjects are chosen on the basis of convenience) is a useful method to use at the beginning of a project as it is inexpensive and practical. This method can also be termed haphazard or accidental sampling. Convenience sampling can be criticized for introducing various types of bias (including researcher bias). However, if you believe that bias is inherent in all types of research, this will be of no more concern than it is with other sampling techniques.

Judgement sampling

This type of sampling can be seen as an extension of the convenience sampling described above. Subjects are chosen because they are seen to be relevant or of interest to the research topic. Again, bias can be introduced but some researchers believe that this is all part of the research process and, as such, should be recognized and acknowledged from the start of the project.

Tip Don't assume that qualitative research is always associated with non-probability (purposive) techniques and quantitative research is associated with probability techniques. This is a false dichotomy that can constrain options and prevent the use of multiple and mixed method approaches.

Choosing Your Sample Size

Choices about sample size will be influenced by your methodology, research topic, budget, available resources and available time. When making choices about sample size, take note of the following advice:

- If your goal is to make generalizations your sample needs to be as large as is possible within your budget and the time available. Statistical methods can be used to choose the size of sample required for a given level of accuracy and the ability to make generalizations (see 'References, Further Reading and Resources' for this chapter at the end of the book).

- When choosing the sample size, make sure that non-response rates are taken into account.

■ If your research requires the use of non-probability sampling techniques, it may be difficult to specify at the beginning of your research how many people you intend to contact. Instead, you continue using your chosen procedure such as snowballing or theoretical sampling until your research question has been answered and no new data are emerging.

■ Be realistic about the size of sample possible on your budget and within your timescale.

Tip For a sample to be useful, it should reflect the similarities and differences found in your study population.

Avoiding Sampling Problems

Choosing and using the correct sampling technique(s) is extremely important. If you get it wrong your whole research project will be compromised. When designing your sample and choosing sampling methods you can overcome problems by taking note of the following advice:

■ Take plenty of time to plan your sampling technique(s). Read all the relevant literature and discuss your plans with your supervisor or an experienced colleague.

■ Ensure that your research population and study population are well defined. Targeting members outside these populations will lead to skewed or biased results. Don't leave out members who are in the research population as this will also lead to biased results.

- If your goal is generalizability, make sure that all members of the study population have an equal chance of being selected. Your sampling method will lead to biased results if some members are favoured over others.

- Use a combination of sampling procedures if it is appropriate for your research.

- Analyse and critique your chosen sampling methods, illustrating why you have made your choice, highlighting any possible concerns and pointing out ways to overcome problems. All this information will be useful for your research proposal (see Chapter 11) and when you come to write your thesis (see Chapter 22).

Tip   A mixed method approach to sampling can help to counteract problems inherent in certain methods and help overcome problems with bias.

Summary

Samples are used in cases where it is impossible or impractical to analyse the whole population. A study population (also called a sampling frame) is chosen and a sample worked out from this. There are two main types of sampling procedure: probability samples and non-probability (purposive) samples. In probability samples, all people within the study population have a specifiable chance of being selected. Non-probability samples, on the other hand, are used if description rather than generalization is the goal.

Now that you understand more about sampling techniques you can apply this understanding to your project and start to choose your participants. The final stage of this planning process is to put all your thoughts into one document (your research proposal). These issues are discussed in the following chapter.

11 Producing a Research Proposal

Producing a research proposal is a vital part of your research. It enables you to write down your ideas and plans and place them in a formal document that can be used to gain funding or for acceptance on to a PhD programme, for example. Your research proposal will cover all the issues discussed in Stages 1 and 2 of this book and will provide a useful document for reference as your research progresses.

This chapter provides information about how to produce a research proposal, including advice on ensuring that you match purpose, audience and style, know how to structure your proposal and understand what makes a good proposal.

Matching Purpose, Audience and Style

When preparing your research proposal, think about the purpose of your research as this will influence the style of your proposal. For example, if you are applying to a funding organization you will need to adhere to rules about style and format, which can include issues such as font size, page length and word count (see Chapter 7). You will also need to follow their guidelines in terms of structure and content.

It is also important to understand the audience when producing your proposal as this will have an influence on the level at which you pitch your work. For example, if the funding organization is staffed by specialists who are experts in your field you can be more technical and spend less time explaining your terms than you would need to do for a lay audience.

Tip   Find out the preferences of funding organizations before you produce your proposal. For example, some funders will want to see that you have expert technical knowledge, whereas others will want to see that you are able to present your research in a way that can be understood by anyone who has an interest in the topic, even if they are not experts.

Producing a PhD research proposal

If you are a postgraduate student you must make sure that your proposal is pitched at the right intellectual level for your audience (the selection panel) and for its purpose (to gain a place on a PhD programme). You will also need to make sure that you follow the structure and style required by your department/university.

A research proposal at PhD level must demonstrate the following:

- you know about, and can critically analyse, current thinking in your discipline;
- you will create and interpret new knowledge (through research and advanced scholarship);
- your work will advance the knowledge in your discipline;
- you are able to design and implement a project that will enable you to generate new knowledge;

- you have the background understanding and required knowledge of relevant research techniques (including an evaluation and critique of methodology and methods);

- you are able to critique, justify and modify your project in light of problems that can arise;

- you will be able to publish your work and it will satisfy peer review.

See also 'Exercise 6: Producing a PhD Research Proposal', below.

Structuring Your Proposal

As we have seen above, proposal structures vary, depending on the needs of your department/funding organization. In general, however, your proposal should include the sections described below.

Title

This should be short and explanatory. It can hint at your research question, your methodology and your research population, e.g. 'Learning Choices: A Grounded Theory Study of Adult Returners'. Brainstorm possible titles and choose the best.

Background

This section should contain a rationale for your research (see Chapter 4). Why are you undertaking the project? Why is the research needed? This discussion should be placed within the context of existing research and/or within your own experience or observation (see Chapter 8). You need to demonstrate that you know what you are talking about and that you have knowledge of the literature surrounding this topic.

If you are unable to find any other research that deals specifically with your proposed project, you need to say so, illustrating how your proposed research will fill this gap and create new knowledge.

Aims and objectives

The aim is the overall driving force of the research and the objectives are the means by which you intend to achieve the aim (see Chapter 5). For a postgraduate project you will need to provide one clear and succinct aim (perhaps with one or two subsidiary aims) and several objectives that relate to your aim(s). Your aims and objectives must relate to your research question and demonstrate how this will be answered.

Methodology

This section describes your proposed research methodology and provides a justification for its use. Why have you decided on this particular methodology and rejected others? How does your proposed methodology relate to your epistemological standpoint and theoretical perspective (see Chapter 1)? Can you foresee any problems with this methodology and how do you intend to overcome them (see Chapter 2)?

If you have chosen a less well-known methodology (or a multiple or mixed approach), you may need to spend more time justifying your choice than you would need to if you had chosen a more traditional methodology. This section of your proposal should be very detailed (many funding organizations report that the most common reason for proposal failure is lack of methodological detail: see 'Reasons for Research Proposal Failure', below).

Research methods

As we have seen in Chapter 9, your research methods are the tools that you intend to use to collect your data and answer your research question. For an advanced research project you need to illustrate how these relate to your methodology and show how these tools are the most appropriate to answer your research question. Why have you decided to use these particular methods? Why are other methods not appropriate? Do you envisage any problems and how do you expect to overcome them?

This section needs to include details about samples, numbers of people to be contacted, methods of data collection, methods of data analysis and ethical considerations.

Timetable

A detailed timetable scheduling all aspects of your research will need to be included in your proposal. This should include the time anticipated for tasks such as conducting background research, questionnaire or interview schedule development and piloting, data collection, data analysis and report writing.

Tip If in doubt about how long a particular task will take, ask an experienced colleague or your supervisor for advice. It is better to overestimate, rather than underestimate (research often takes longer than anticipated).

Budget and resources

This is an important section for researchers who intend to apply for funding for their project. It is perhaps less important for postgraduate students, although your supervisor might require some information about how much you expect your project to cost and the resources you will need.

If you are intending to apply for funding, obtain the most up-to-date guidelines about producing a budget and costing your project (see Chapter 6). All funding organizations will only meet acceptable costs and all will want to see value for money in terms of strategic importance and research impact (see Chapter 7).

Research impact

Funding organizations and universities are interested in research impact (defined by Research Councils UK as 'the demonstrable contribution that excellent research makes to society and the economy'). You need to think about the intended impact of your own research and describe this in detail in this section of your proposal.

For some researchers this is both difficult and controversial. However, for most funding organizations it is a necessity. Your university research office will be able to offer further advice if you struggle with this section.

Dissemination

This section demonstrates how you intend to let others know about the results of your research. This can be through producing a thesis and providing a copy for the university library, journal papers (including deposits in open access repositories), conference papers, internal and external seminars, blogs, lectures, monographs, chapters for books and entire books, for example.

References and bibliography

Your reference section should contain all the literature to which you have referred in your proposal and the bibliography should contain all other relevant literature. Referencing software will help you to produce these sections quickly and efficiently (see Chapter 8).

Exercise 6: Producing a PhD Research Proposal

Produce your PhD research proposal following the guidelines offered above. Once you have done this, critically analyse your proposal ensuring that it meets the required criteria for a PhD proposal (listed above), that it meets the criteria for a good proposal (described below) and that you have avoided all the reasons for proposal failure (listed below).

Producing a Good Proposal

To produce a good research proposal you must make sure that your research is unique and/or offers new insight or development, with useful policy and practice implications, and demonstrable impact. It must be relevant (to the work of the funding body or to your course, for example). The aims and objectives must be clear and succinct and illustrate how you intend to answer your research question.

You will need to demonstrate that thorough background research and a comprehensive literature review have taken place (unless your methodology suggests that this is not appropriate) and that you have relevant background knowledge and/or experience. The timetable, resources and budget will need to be described in detail, with all eventualities covered.

An awareness of why research projects fail will help you to avoid common pitfalls and help you to produce a good research proposal (see 'Reasons for Research Proposal Failure', below).

Reasons for Research Proposal Failure

■ The aims and objectives are unclear or vague.

■ There is no connection between epistemological standpoint, theoretical perspective and methodological position.

■ There is a mismatch between the approach being adopted and the issues to be addressed.

■ The overall plan is too ambitious and difficult to achieve in the timescale, or the proposed timescale is inappropriate or unrealistic.

■ The researcher has not conducted enough in-depth background research.

■ The research question is of insufficient importance.

■ Information about the data collection method(s) is insufficiently detailed.

■ Information about the data analysis method(s) is insufficiently detailed.

■ Resources and budget have not been carefully thought out.

■ The researcher is asking for too much money without justification.

■ The topic is not original enough.

Summary

Your research proposal is an important document that provides a detailed description of your proposed research. Proposals can vary in terms of structure and style, depending on the purpose and audience. Although proposals can vary, in general they will include a title, background, aims and objectives, methodology, research methods, timetable, budget and resources, research impact, dissemination, and references and bibliography. A good proposal should be clear, well written, well justified in terms of topic and method, and have a clear timetable and well-developed budget.

Once your research proposal has been accepted (and funding obtained, if relevant), you can go on to conduct your research. These issues are discussed in the next stage of this book.

STAGE 3

CONDUCTING YOUR RESEARCH

12 Running Focus Groups

A focus group is a collection of interacting individuals, with common characteristics or interests, holding a discussion that is introduced and led by a moderator. Focus groups can be used as a research method by researchers approaching their work from different epistemological and methodological standpoints, although care must be taken to ensure compatibility of method with underlying standpoint.

The aim of a focus group is not to reach consensus: instead, it is to gain a greater understanding of attitudes, opinions, beliefs, behaviour and perceptions (with the focus on interaction as part of the research data). This chapter illustrates how focus groups are used in different types of research and provides practical information about how to arrange and run a focus group.

A Feminist Postmodernist View of Focus Groups

From a feminist postmodernist view, focus groups can be seen to be an important method to use in the advancement of an agenda for social justice. This is because they can 'serve to expose and validate women's everyday experiences of subjugation and their individual and collective survival and resistance strategies' (Madriz 2003: 364).

Understanding the Uses of Focus Groups

There are various ways that focus groups can be used for an advanced research project, as the examples below illustrate.

Example 1

A researcher who is undertaking an action research project decides to use focus groups at the planning (diagnostic) stage of the project to find out what people think about being part of the project, what they hope to gain and what changes they would like to see.

Another focus group is held with the participants halfway through the project. The researcher thinks that a group opinion at this stage will be helpful, but also decides to interview some key participants on an individual basis. This will help the researcher to understand more about group dynamics and the influence of social interaction.

A final focus group is held at the end of the project, during a process of evaluation, to find out what people think about having been part of the project. Also, the researcher wants the group to develop some recommendations for continuing with change once the researcher has left the group.

Example 2

A researcher has developed some interesting themes that have emerged from semi-structured interviews with individuals during a grounded theory study. She thinks that it might be interesting to discuss these further with other people from the study population. She arranges five focus groups, selecting participants using a theoretical sampling technique (see Chapter 10). The emerging themes are discussed and refined in light of the focus-group data. Existing literature is also used to explain the emerging themes further.

At the end of the project the researcher has developed her theory based on the themes and concepts that have emerged from the data. To improve the reliability of her work she decides to find out whether her theory is credible and believable from the perspective of the participants. Five more focus groups are arranged and the theory is modified in light of the discussions.

Example 3

A researcher has just analysed a closed-ended questionnaire that had been sent out to a sample of the study population. However, he is baffled by the responses in one section. In an attempt to understand the responses he arranges a focus group with a sample of people from the study population. He discusses the issues and is able to gain a deeper understanding of the data.

Tip Don't assume that focus groups cannot be used for sensitive topics. Participants can help other group members through their embarrassment, provide mutual support and help each other to express opinions or describe difficult personal experiences. Issues of confidentiality and anonymity will need to be addressed (see Chapter 27).

Arranging a Focus Group

When arranging a focus group you need to think about your sample, participants, venue and method of recording, as described below.

Your sample

Choose your sample carefully (see Chapter 10). Your participants should be drawn only from your study population. Care must be taken to avoid bias in the selection process; for example, choosing participants because others believe they will be 'good' participants, or allowing a person in a position of authority to select the group members for you (such as an employer selecting employees).

Your participants

Nine or eleven participants is the ideal number (odd numbers work better than even numbers as it is harder for participants to pair up and hold breakaway conversations). Over-recruit by a small number if you feel some participants may drop out. Give plenty of notice about time and venue, and contact your participants the day before to check that they have remembered and can still attend.

Your participants should have something in common (this will be the focus of your research) and they should feel comfortable talking with each other and speaking in a group setting. Be aware of how group compositions can silence minority voices or censor sensitive information. You must also be aware of systemic bias (the shared beliefs of those who participate) and systematic bias (how the participants work together).

Your venue

Choose your venue carefully. Is it accessible, both mentally and physically? Will the participants feel comfortable accessing the venue? Are they familiar with the location? Do they know where to go? Is the room easy to find? Is there someone there to welcome them and tell them what to expect? Is parking available and/or is it close to public transport?

Make sure that your venue is free from distractions and disturbances. Arrive early to arrange the furniture to suit your participants (boardroom style for business executives, an informal horseshoe style for counsellors, for example).

Your method of recording

Choose a good-quality digital recording device that has a microphone powerful enough to pick up every voice in the room (see Chapter 16). Check that there is a suitable surface on which to place equipment, equidistant from all participants. Power and recording lights are useful so that you can check (discreetly) that the equipment is working and recording during the discussion.

Tip Participants in focus groups tend to speak quietly at the beginning, but once they begin to relax, they tend to raise their voices. You need to make sure that your recorder picks up all the discussion. Be aware of any noise that could disrupt the recorder, such as ticking clocks or traffic outside.

Running a Focus Group

A good focus group should be run in the following way:

1. Greet participants as they arrive and provide them with your chosen refreshments (think carefully about whether to provide alcohol and, if you do, don't provide too much). Place refreshments away from the discussion area (and recording device).

2. Introduce yourself, explain why you are holding the discussion and tell participants what will happen to the results.

3. Assure the participants about anonymity and confidentiality, asking also that they respect this and do not pass on what has been said in the group to third parties (see Chapter 27).

4. Before you start the discussion, negotiate a suitable time with the participants and ask that everyone respects this as it can be very disruptive having people come in late or leave early. One and a half hours is an ideal length, although some focus groups may last a lot longer.

5. Ask the participants to respect each other. Only one person should speak at a time, they should not interrupt each other, no one person should dominate and all opinions should be seen as valid, even if others might not agree with them.

6. Begin with general, easy questions to help people relax. Listen to all responses and jot down notes about issues to which you would like to return. Don't be afraid of silence: someone else will fill the gap.

7. Make sure that no one person dominates and try to ensure that all participants have a chance to speak, although you shouldn't cajole someone into offering an opinion if they do not wish to do so.

8. As moderator your aim is to get a free-flowing discussion so that you have less input, although you need to make sure that the discussion remains on topic.

9. When you have finished your focus group, thank the participants for taking part and leave a contact name and number in case they wish to follow up any of the issues that have been raised during the discussion. You may find that people are willing to stay longer than the negotiated time, if they have enjoyed themselves. If this is the case you should make it clear that those who want to leave can do so.

Tip You may find it useful to negotiate a code of behaviour with your participants. They will raise issues such as dominance, aggression, abuse, not listening, interrupting and so on. If this code has been negotiated by participants themselves, they tend to be more willing to adhere to it during the discussion.

Summary

Focus groups are used in a variety of research projects to gain a more in-depth opinion from participants and to understand processes of social interaction. They can be used in an exploratory way, for example, to help inform a questionnaire, or they can be used towards the end of a project to help explain emerging themes. Participants are chosen from the study population, using a variety of sampling techniques (depending on methodology). The discussion is introduced and facilitated by a moderator, who makes sure that the discussion stays on topic. The moderator also controls break-away conversations, dominance and disruption.

Focus groups provide the opportunity to speak to a group of people at the same time, enabling participants to bounce thoughts and ideas off each other and provide mutual support. If, however, it is more appropriate to research individual opinion, one-to-one interviews are used. This method is discussed in the following chapter.

13 Conducting Interviews

Interviews are a popular method of data collection used by researchers from all epistemological and methodological standpoints. For example, structured interviews can be used by those approaching their work from an objectivist standpoint; unstructured (or life-history) interviews can be used by those approaching their work from a constructionist standpoint; and discursive and conversational analysis of interview data can be employed by those approaching their work from a subjectivist standpoint (see Chapter 1).

This chapter provides information about using interviews in social research, knowing about the different types of interview, producing an interview schedule, conducting interviews and recording interviews.

Using Interviews in Social Research

The way that interviews are used in social research depends on your epistemological and methodological standpoint. It also depends on your theoretical perspective, as the following examples illustrate.

▪ From a positivist perspective researchers seek to understand and describe a particular phenomenon. Structured interviews can be used as part of a large-scale survey to obtain attitudes and beliefs about a particular topic (see 'Structured interviews', below). Emphasis is placed on neutrality, technical detail and ensuring that experiential knowledge is transmitted from the interviewee to the interviewer.

- Within phenomenology researchers are interested in finding out how participants experience life-world phenomena. Life-world interviews (unstructured, in-depth interviews) can be used to obtain a concrete description of the lived world in a person's own words. The interview is reciprocal and informal.

- Within hermeneutics researchers are interested in searching for essential meanings connected with everyday human experiences. The researcher (being intimately connected to the research question) creates an atmosphere of engagement and connection during extended interviews. This encourages participants to express and explore meanings that are within their experience.

- Within postmodernism the focus is on the construction of social meaning through language and discursive practices. Postmodern interviewing is a conversation with diverse purposes, where interview roles are flexible and ever-changing. Different techniques are adopted, depending on postmodernist standpoint (see 'Postmodern interviews' below).

Tip An understanding of the connections between epistemology, theoretical perspective and methodology is vital when deciding on what type of interview is most appropriate for your research (see Chapters 1, 2 and 9). This is because your standpoint will influence the type of interview, the focus of the interview, the method used and the way that the interview is analysed.

Knowing About the Different Types of Interview

As we have seen above, there are many different types of interview that can be used in social research. Some are used to gather descriptive data whereas others seek to obtain a wider, holistic view of lived experience. Different types of interview create different types of data and different forms of knowledge. Also, transcripts can be analysed in very different ways. The various types of interview are listed below. For a fuller discussion, see 'References, Further Reading and Resources' for this chapter at the end of the book.

Structured interviews

Structured interviews are used in survey research to ask the same set of standardized questions to all respondents in the same order. The questions are grouped into predetermined categories that will help to answer the research question, or confirm/disconfirm the hypothesis. The assumption is that the respondent has experiential knowledge that can be transmitted to the interviewer. Interview data can be analysed and, if correct procedures have been followed, generalizations can be made to the target population.

Semi-structured interviews

Semi-structured interviews are used to ask standard questions of each respondent but also allow for additional questions and probing for detail, if required. The assumption is that experiential knowledge can be transmitted from the respondent to the researcher, and that there may be additional themes/experiences that have not been predetermined by the researcher. Although some engagement is required, the researcher does not become personally involved. Data can be quantified and compared and contrasted with data from other interviews.

Unstructured interviews

Unstructured interviews provide the freedom for people to tell their life stories in a way that they wish, with the researcher helping to keep the narrative moving forward. The emphasis is on finding meanings and acquiring a deep understanding of people's life experiences. As such, this type of interview may require considerable personal disclosure from the inter- viewee. Life-story interviews and oral-history interviews (described below) are two types of unstructured interview.

Life-story interviews

Life-story interviews cover the whole life story of the inter- viewee, told in their own words, in their own way, with little directional input from the researcher. The interviewee chooses how and in what order to present their personal nar- rative, and they may also choose to include a clarification and justification for life experiences.

The researcher can explore specific social, cultural and histor- ical issues within the life story, consider connections between the life story and wider public events and compare life stories (within families or through similar experiences, for example).

Oral-history interviews

Oral-history interviews record bibliographic accounts of peo- ple's lives. They concentrate on a particular period in a person's life to obtain a first-hand account of experiences during the historical period that is of interest. The researcher encourages the interviewee to provide their account in their own words, but steers the narrative back on course if it veers from the topic. The researcher is interested in what the interviewee perceives to be true, rather than in the collection of facts.

Feminist interviews

Feminist interviews are conducted in a co-constructive, non-hierarchical, reciprocal and reflexive manner. Women are encouraged to provide their own accounts in their own words with the interviewer only serving as a guide (or as a partner). Issues of rapport, trust, empathy and respect are highlighted. An awareness of gender relations is important during data collection and analysis.

Theoretical perspective and methodological standpoint have an influence on the type and structure of feminist interview (a feminist postmodernist will have a very different style of interview from a feminist empiricist, for example).

Postmodern interviews

Postmodern interviews attempt to minimize researcher input, influence and interpretation during the interview process. However, there is not a standard type of postmodern interview. Instead, experimentation with, and new imaginings of, the interview method are seen to be desirable. For example, researchers can adopt creative interviewing techniques (mutual disclosure, cooperation and intimacy) or critical interviewing techniques (considering the influence of social, cultural, historic and economic factors on reported experience).

Producing an Interview Schedule

An interview schedule is a list of topics and/or questions that are to be discussed in the interview. Whether you choose to use a list of topics or questions depends on your methodology and personal preference. Indeed, some researchers approaching their work from a postmodernist perspective, for example, may decide not to use an interview schedule at all.

If you do decide to use an interview schedule, the following advice will help:

- Brainstorm your research topic. Write down every topic you can think of without analysis or judgement.

- Work through your list carefully, discarding irrelevant topics and grouping similar suggestions.

- Categorize each suggestion under a list of more general topics.

- Order these general topics into a logical sequence, leaving sensitive or controversial issues until the end. Move from general to specific.

- Think of questions relating to each of these general topics. Ask about experience and behaviour before asking about opinion and feelings.

- When developing questions, make sure they are open rather than closed (unless you are producing questions for a structured interview). Keep questions short and to the point. Use language that will be understood by your participants. Avoid jargon and double-barrelled questions (two questions in one).

- Become familiar with your interview schedule so that your interview can flow smoothly.

■ Revise your schedule after each interview (if this fits with your chosen methodology).

Tip Practise questions with friends and colleagues to make sure that the questions can be understood, are relevant and can be answered easily. This will help you to iron out ambiguity.

Conducting an Interview

The following advice is relevant for most types of social research interview:

■ Choose a suitable venue. This should be a safe place to meet and will need to be accessible to your participants (both mentally and physically). It should be warm, comfortable and free from disturbances and distractions.

■ Dress and behave in a way appropriate for the interview.

■ Establish rapport. Don't rush into the interview, unless the participant is happy to do so. Make conversation, accept a cup of tea and treat the participant with courtesy and respect.

■ Negotiate a time at the beginning. Stick to this time, although you will probably find that the participant is happy to continue, if they are enjoying the interview.

■ Introduce yourself and explain the purpose of your research. Let the participant know what will happen to the results. Discuss issues of confidentiality and anonymity (see Chapter 27).

■ Maintain eye contact and show an interest in everything that is said.

- Listen carefully to responses, jotting down issues to which you may wish to return and probe for more information (if your methodology allows this).

- Summarize what interviewees have said as a way of finding out if you have understood them and to determine whether they wish to add any further information (if your methodology allows this).

- Achieve closure, thank them and leave a contact number or email address in case they wish to get in touch with you about anything that has arisen.

- Respect confidentiality (don't pass on what has been said to third parties unless you have requested permission to do so).

Recording Your Interview

The best way to record your interview is to use a high-quality digital recording device. Most interviewees are now comfortable with this type of technology and will not object. However, always take a pen and paper with you to the interview, just in case someone does not want to be recorded. Also, it is useful to jot down notes as the interview progresses so that you can return to pertinent points. If you have taken notes at any stage during the interview, write them up as soon as you can after the interview.

Become familiar with the recording equipment before your interviews and check the batteries. Place the recorder on a non-vibratory surface, between you and the participant. A power and recording light is useful so that you can check, discreetly, that it is still recording as the interview progresses. Check that there are no noises that can disrupt or disturb the recording. Explain exactly what will happen to the recording, who will hear it, how the recording will be stored and when it will be deleted. More information about recording and storing data is provided in Chapter 16.

Tip If you are asking for considerable personal disclosure, or if your topic is of a sensitive nature, you may need to volunteer to turn off the recorder for part of the interview.

Summary

There are various types of interview that are used in social research, including structured, semi-structured and unstructured interviews. The type of interview that you use, and the way that you analyse your data, depends on your epistemological and methodological standpoint, theoretical perspective and personal preference. When conducting interviews you must act ethically, establish rapport, treat your participants with respect and pay close attention to issues of anonymity, confidentiality and data protection.

Interviews provide the opportunity to obtain individual information from each participant. Another popular social research method that is used to gather data from individual participants is the questionnaire. This is discussed in the next chapter.

14 Using Questionnaires

Questionnaires are a popular data collection method used by researchers from different epistemological and methodological standpoints. For example, open-ended questionnaires are typically used in qualitative research (from a constructionist standpoint, for example), and structured, closed-ended questionnaires are used in quantitative research (from an objectivist standpoint). Questionnaires can be self-administered or researcher-administered in a variety of ways such as face-to-face, over the telephone, through the post or online.

This chapter provides information about using questionnaires in social research, offering advice about designing and administering a questionnaire and ensuring that you get a high response rate.

Using Questionnaires in Social Research

Questionnaires are used to gather data about behaviour, experiences, attitudes, beliefs and values. They must be well constructed and analysed correctly so that the data are reliable and can lead to valid conclusions. For objectivists who hope to describe an objective truth, a stimulus-response model is employed, with standardized questions and answers being the favoured approach for large-scale surveys (see 'Surveys that Use Questionnaires: Objectivist Standpoint' box below). Validity and reliability are extremely important when designing this type of questionnaire and when interpreting data.

Researchers who approach questionnaire design from the constructionist standpoint, however, stress that both questions and answers have to be understood in terms of the social contexts in which they operate. Since it is meaning (and the construction of meaning) that is important, the questionnaire design and the way it is administered is very different. The researcher plays a much more important role in helping to construct meaning and, as such, questionnaires can be flexible and fluid.

Surveys that Use Questionnaires: Objectivist Standpoint

There are three main types of survey that use questionnaires from an objectivist standpoint.

Cross-sectional surveys are used to describe attitudes and behaviour at one point in time. They tend to be exploratory and descriptive, but can also be used to find correlations and make predictions. They cannot assess changes over time or give insights into the causes of population characteristics.

Longitudinal surveys set out to explore and describe what is happening over time (over months or years, through the use of two or more discrete surveys). There are two main types of longitudinal survey. 'Cohort surveys' (or 'panel surveys') follow the same group of individuals, with a common characteristic or experience, over time. 'Trend surveys' ask the same questions to different respondents within the study population over a period of time.

Successive independent sample surveys are similar to the trend surveys described above (some researchers use the terms interchangeably). These surveys use multiple random samples from the same (equally representative) population at one or more times. The same questions are asked so that results can be compared. These surveys seek to study changes in attitudes of the population (but not changes within individuals).

Designing a Questionnaire

Despite these very different approaches, there are some practical issues about questionnaire design that are pertinent to most approaches, as detailed below.

- Your questionnaire should be as short as possible. Produce straightforward, clear and short questions. Don't ask unnecessary questions or any that are not relevant to your research topic. Include filter questions that enable respondents to skip sections that are not relevant to them.

- Start with easy-to-answer questions. Keep complex questions for the end.

- Don't assume knowledge or make it seem that you expect a certain level of knowledge by the way your questions are worded.

- Make sure that your questions don't contain some type of prestige bias (questions that could embarrass or force respondents into giving a false answer).

- Don't create opinions artificially by asking someone a question they know nothing about or they don't care about.

- Avoid jargon and technical words and don't use words that have multiple meanings.

- Avoid double-barrelled questions, negative questions and leading questions.

- Don't cause offence, frustration, sadness or anger, and ensure that you avoid words with emotional connotations.

- Don't ask people to guess how others would feel, unless it is a sensitive topic that would work better this way (some issues may be very sensitive and you might be better asking an indirect question rather than a direct question).

- Avoid vague words such as 'often' and 'sometimes'. Use specific time frames when asking about behaviour. Also, use specific place frames.

- Provide all possible responses in a closed question and consider all alternatives (see 'Case Study: Claire', below). Make sure that all frequencies/time frames are supplied, if you are using them.

Case Study: Claire

I was filling in a questionnaire about eating healthy food. The questions were all about how much fresh and frozen fruit and vegetables I buy from my local supermarket. They asked what I bought, how often and whether I preferred packaged, pre-cut, pre-prepared or pre-cooked fruit and vegetables.

For every answer I had to tick 'not applicable – I don't buy fresh fruit and vegetables'. What do the researchers get from that answer? Do they presume I am very unhealthy and live on take-away foods? Actually, I have an allotment and grow all my own fruit and veg. I am completely self-sufficient and have a very healthy diet. But their questionnaire didn't allow for this response and the answers I had to provide will give completely the wrong impression about my eating habits.

Administering a Questionnaire

The way that you administer your questionnaire will have an influence on the format and design. For example, do you intend to use a self-administered questionnaire or an interview-administered questionnaire? If the former is the case you must ensure that respondents can read (and read the English language) before administering the questionnaire. If the latter is the case, you need to decide how many interviewers are to be used and think about how you intend to ensure continuity (if relevant to your methodology).

The number of questionnaires and the method of distribution depend on your chosen sampling technique (see Chapter 10). For example, if you are intending to carry out a large-scale survey you can distribute self-administered questionnaires by post, in person (time and resources permitting) or online. Smaller numbers of open-ended questionnaires, on the other hand, could be distributed face-to-face, or by a 'gatekeeper' (a relevant person within the organization who has been given concise instructions), for example.

When administering a questionnaire you must introduce yourself, explain the purpose of the research and let respondents know what will happen to the results (this can be either written or done verbally). It is important to raise the issues of confidentiality, anonymity and data protection (see Chapter 27). Always be honest about how long the questionnaire will take to complete. Give a specific deadline for return and send out a reminder letter/questionnaire in cases of non-response.

Tip There is no one right way to go about designing and administering a questionnaire in the social sciences. This is because there are different approaches that depend on your epistemological and methodological standpoint, research question, aims and objectives, target population, budget and resources. However, there are many ways that you can go wrong, so it is imperative that you read around the subject, understand what you are doing, carefully construct your questionnaire, pilot (test) the questions and refine as appropriate.

Ensuring a High Response Rate

You can improve your response rate by making sure that each of the following questions is answered when you design and administer your questionnaire:

- Is your questionnaire relevant to the lives, attitudes and beliefs of the respondents? Are your intended respondents likely to cooperate? For example, illegal immigrants may be less likely to fill in a questionnaire than legal immigrants. Can your respondents see some personal benefit to be gained by completing the questionnaire?

- Are the instructions straightforward and have you been realistic about how long it will take to complete?

- Have the respondents been told who the research is for and what will happen to the results? Have they been assured that you understand and will comply with the Data Protection Act?

- Is your questionnaire interesting and is it easy to follow? Is it well constructed and well laid out? Is it clear, concise and uncluttered? Layout and spacing are extremely important. If your questionnaire looks cluttered, respondents will be less likely to fill it in.

- Is return postage included (if relevant)?

- Has a follow-up letter and duplicate questionnaire been sent in cases of non-response?

Exercise 7: Producing and Piloting a Questionnaire

Design your questionnaire following the guidelines provided in this chapter. Make sure that your questionnaire fits with your epistemological and methodological standpoint (see Chapters 1 and 2), that it addresses your research question (see Chapter 3) and that all questions are relevant to your aims and objectives (see Chapter 5).

Once you have designed your questionnaire, ask your supervisor/work colleague for comments. Pilot your questionnaire with a sample of your research population. Once you have done this you will be able to get an idea about expected response rates, data quality, data validity and reliability, and the comprehensibility of questions. Modify your questionnaire accordingly.

Summary

Questionnaires are used by social researchers to gather data on attitudes, beliefs, experiences and opinions. The type, design and analysis of questionnaires depend on your epistemological and methodological standpoint. For example, objectivists might seek an objective truth through large-scale, closed-question surveys, and constructionists might highlight the social and cultural contexts of questions and answers. Whatever your standpoint, there are certain basic rules that you should follow when designing and administering a questionnaire, such as avoiding jargon and not asking double-barrelled, negative or leading questions.

This section of the book has discussed focus groups, interviews and questionnaires. The next chapter goes on to offer advice about collecting data through participant observation (which can employ all these methods so far described).

15 Becoming a Participant Observer

Participant observation is a method used to study a group of people within a particular social and cultural environment. It is a procedure for generating understanding about the way of life of others. Participant observation can be viewed as a methodology, rather than a method, as it took shape within particular historical and social circumstances in anthropology and sociology (where important methodological issues were raised). However, as there are many practical 'how to' issues involved in the use of participant observation, it can also be viewed as a research method.

This chapter shows how participant observation is used in social research, highlighting the importance of building trust and gaining access, illustrating how data are collected and analysed and discussing issues of ethics and completing the study.

Using Participant Observation in Social Research

Participant observation is a method used by ethnographers who provide interpretive and descriptive analyses of the symbolic and other meanings that inform the routine practices of everyday life. Within ethnography there are different traditions, such as reflexive or critical ethnography (involving an ideological critique and questioning the status quo of power relations) and naturalistic ethnography (founded on positivism and based on the legacy of colonialism). These different traditions influence the way that participant observation is conducted and data are analysed.

Participant observation can be carried out within any community, culture or context. The researcher immerses themselves into the community: the action is deliberate and intended to add to knowledge. Various research methods are used during the study. These can include life-story interviews (see Chapter 13), focus-group discussions (see Chapter 12) and analysis of personal documents, for example. Although most participant observation is qualitative in nature, some researchers will employ quantitative techniques (such as coding and counting responses) where appropriate, depending on the methodological standpoint.

There are five main stages to a participant observation study: gaining access, working in the field, collecting data, analysing data and withdrawing from the field, as described below.

Tip Your epistemological standpoint and theoretical perspective will inform decisions about ethnographic type and method, and help you to decide whether participant observation is appropriate. For example, feminists and postmodernists might point out the limitations of the method, illustrating how observations are dependent on what participants are willing to share and arguing that all accounts (participants' and observers') are fabrications. Researchers approaching from this standpoint might concede that participants have a view (which can be better than no view), but that participant observation should be treated with caution and only used together with other methods.

Gaining Access

As a researcher you have to be trusted before you can gain access to a particular group. This involves a careful process of establishing contacts, meeting with people, establishing rapport and being accepted. This can be difficult if the group is disparate: although you might gain acceptance by some members of the group, this might not be the case for all members. Factions can cause problems and you must have a good knowledge and understanding of group dynamics before entering the field.

You can employ a 'gatekeeper' to help you gain access. This is a person within the group who is willing to accept you and introduce you to other members as part of the group. Problems can arise if the gatekeeper is not chosen carefully (e.g. they are not trusted or hold little respect within the group).

Working in the Field

Once access has been gained you need to work hard to be accepted by all group members. Researchers can cause suspicion, especially if some members do not understand why you wish to join their group. You need to dress, speak, behave and act appropriately and must not appear threatening, superior or untrustworthy. In the early stages it is important to answer all questions honestly, rather than try to avoid them.

In a participant observation study you participate in the community while observing others within that community (this can happen at different levels; see 'Tip', below). You will need to be a researcher twenty-four hours a day for a significant period of time, which can be physically exhausting and mentally challenging.

Tip There are different levels of participation: it is important to think about how much of a participant observer you wish to be. For example, you could become a complete participant (this could occur if you are already a member of the group under study, for example). Or you could choose to be a passive participant, observing but not taking part in group activities. On the other hand, you could participate in an active way, fully embracing the activities of the group but not actually becoming a complete member.

Collecting Data

All researchers ask questions. However, a participant observation study differs from other research methods in that, at the beginning of a study, it is often better not to ask questions. This is because you may not know what is important in the early stages. Other members of the group may, instead, approach you and ask questions, which in itself can provide important data. Also, issues that may appear to be important at the start of the project can become much less significant later.

Field notes are the main way of recording data. These can be practical details about events, times, dates and places, or they can be methodological notes concerning your role and influence on the encounter, or observations on what a specific encounter might mean, for example. Your notes can also highlight discrepancies between what people say and what they do.

It is useful to keep a day-to-day diary in addition to all the other field notes. You also need to keep all transcripts of interviews, photographs, maps, tapes, video recordings, diagrams and plans. Everything needs to be recorded and stored systematically, so good organizational skills are important for participant observation studies.

Tip You may find it useful to keep a journal in which you reflect on your own gender, ethnicity, age, sexual orientation and experiences, and how these influence your research, what you observe and how you record your observations.

Analysing Data

A preliminary analysis is undertaken as data are collected (through coding and classifying notes, for example). Themes are developed or hypotheses formed that you can discuss, check and refine with informants. This process of data collection and analysis continues throughout your study. Data from other sources can be incorporated into the analysis to help explain emerging themes. All inferences have to be backed up with evidence, so you must continue with data collection until there is enough evidence available.

Various types of data analysis techniques can be employed, such as thematic and narrative analysis, coding and counting. Choice of analysis technique depends on the type of data-collection methods that have been used and on your personal preferences and methodological standpoint (see Chapters 18 and 19).

Withdrawing from the Field

As we have seen above, most data analysis takes place in the field so that hypotheses can be checked and verified. Key informants are used to help with this verification. As you move through this process it gradually becomes evident that no new themes are emerging and that you have a good understanding of the group under study. In most cases it becomes clear that the time is right to withdraw from the field and write up results.

Some researchers find this a very difficult process and may delay the decision for as long as possible (time and resources permitting). However, you can make this transition easier by keeping in contact with informants and agreeing to return at a later date, perhaps when the report is published, for example.

It is extremely important to leave the group on good terms and ensure that informants have had a positive experience. This will be of benefit if you wish to return at a later date for a follow-up study and it helps to create positive perceptions about researchers in general.

Knowing About Ethical Issues

The nature of participant observation means that there are many ethical issues that need to be addressed before, during and after the fieldwork. If you are thinking about this type of study you should consider the following questions.

Before:

- Are you prepared to spend many months studying others and not indulging in talk about yourself?

- If you are going to mix with people who have very different social and political beliefs, can you remain neutral and keep your opinions to yourself? Indeed, is this desirable? Your thoughts on this will be guided by your epistemological standpoint and theoretical perspective.

- Are you prepared for the emergence of as yet unconscious emotional factors? You may find out things about yourself that you do not like, especially in terms of your own prejudices.

- Will your contact be traumatic or upsetting? If so, can you handle this?

During:

- If the group is suspicious, do you intend to be completely honest about who you are and what you are doing? Are you prepared to lie if it means you can gain access? How would you deal with any problems that may arise due to your deception?

- Will you be expected to do anything illegal? Are you prepared to break the law and are you able to put up with any consequences that could arise as a result of your activities?

- Some people will not accept you. Are you prepared for rejection and can you handle it when it happens? Are you able to banish rejection anxieties from the outset?

After:

- What if your participation within a group has caused problems, anxieties or arguments amongst other members? Do you know how to deal with the situation? Are you prepared to withdraw and ruin all your hard work for the sake of your informants?

- Are you prepared to be used as a scapegoat if things go wrong within the community under study?

- Have you taken great care to ensure that there will not be repercussions for any member of the group due to their involvement in your study?

Summary

Participant observation is a research method that is used in the social sciences and anthropology to study groups of people in a particular social situation. Using this method the researcher lives among the group, participating in activities while observing behaviour. Field notes are taken and analysed, and data gathered using a variety of research methods such as interviews, group discussions and analysis of personal records.

Recording and storing data is an extremely important part of a participant observation study (and is an important activity for all social researchers). These issues are discussed in the following chapter.

16 Recording and Storing Data

Recording and storing data is an essential part of your research, so it is important that you make the right decisions in the planning stages of your work. Advances in digital technology have made audio- and video-recording devices accessible and affordable to social researchers, while well-designed software enables easy and convenient editing, copying, analysis and storage of digital data.

This chapter illustrates how decisions about recording methods are influenced by epistemology, methodology and theoretical perspective. It goes on to provide practical information about choosing and using suitable recording equipment, storing data and complying with data protection regulations.

Recording Methods in Social Research

As an advanced social researcher your decisions about recording methods will need to fit with your epistemological and methodological standpoint and your theoretical perspective (see Chapters 1 and 2). For example, positivists seeking an objective truth may decide to record responses from a structured interview on a standardized form that has been grouped into predetermined categories and responses. Postmodernists, on the other hand, may pay close attention to recording visual and auditory signals, and asking for an interpretation of these, during an extended interview. For these researchers, recording body language and non-verbal communication is seen to be as important as the interview transcript itself.

Video can help researchers who approach their work from constructionist and subjectivist standpoints by providing the opportunity to capture the context and action of the social event. Using video can help to highlight the non-verbal cues and actions of human behaviour and communication, and enable interpretation by multiple viewers. Although the focus of the observation may be social interaction, there is also the interaction (and influence) of the researcher with video camera to be considered.

Tip When making decisions about recording technology, it is important to make sure that it is suitable, in practical terms, for your chosen participants. For example, although most people are familiar with audio and video technology, they may not want to be recorded or identified on film if they are part of a secretive society or engaging in unlawful behaviour.

Choosing Suitable Audio Equipment

There is a wide variety of affordable, good-quality audio devices available for social researchers. It is easy to edit, store and back-up digital interview recordings, and software is available to enable you to attach metadata to digital recordings (e.g. copyright, ownership and contextual data).

If you decide that audio recording is suitable for your chosen methodology, there are various points to consider when choosing your equipment:

- Choose the most durable and dependable recording equipment that you can afford. Make sure that there is enough memory (internal and external) for your needs.

- Make sure that the recorder has a light or display that indicates when the power (either mains or battery) is working.

- Check that there is a light or display that indicates that the recording function is working and that the recording sound level is adequate.

- Choose a recorder that has an output terminal (such as a USB port) that enables you to transfer sound files direct to your computer.

- Make sure that the internal microphone is adequate for your needs. Most are very good, but if you are running a large focus group, for example, you might need to consider using an external microphone. Therefore, you will need to choose a recorder that has an input for connecting external audio signals (the type of input provided by the recorder will determine what type of microphone can be connected).

Tip If you have to travel to a lot of interviews and intend to use your recorder in a variety of situations, buy a durable, solid case to keep your equipment safe. You will also need to buy extra batteries and memory cards and always take them with you when recording in the field.

Choosing Suitable Video Equipment

Digital video technology has also moved on rapidly (and prices have reduced considerably) so that this recording option is becoming a more popular and accessible method for social researchers. If you have access to university video equipment and/or video-recording suites you can ask your IT technician about capabilities and operation.

If you need to buy your own equipment, there are various points that you need to consider when making your choices:

- Decide whether you intend to video with a handheld device, use a tripod, or use both methods, as this will influence the size, weight and type of video camera. If you intend to hold your camera, make sure it has good image stability (find out how comfortable it is in your hand, check that the weight is right and make sure that you can access the controls easily without much movement).

- Are you undertaking overt or covert filming? Again, this will have a big influence on the size and style of recorder. Ethics must be considered when making these decisions (see Chapter 27).

- Make sure the camera has a USB port for transferring video to your computer, for viewing, editing, analysis and storage.

- Check the quality of the microphone. You may need to fit an external microphone in cases where handling and background noises affect the recording, so check that a socket is available.

- Buy your camera from a reputable source and buy the best that you can afford. Check that there is a suitable warranty. A returns policy is useful if you find that the camera is not suitable for your needs.

Using Recording Devices

When using recording equipment in your research it is important to obtain permission first. Although most Western societies are now familiar with recording equipment and feel comfortable with its use, there are some societies that are suspicious of the technology and do not feel comfortable. If this is the case you may have to take notes instead. In most cases you should not undertake covert recording of any kind. It gives researchers a bad name and is ethically unsound (see Chapter 27).

It is important to give an explanation about what will happen to the recording, which should cover the following:

- how and where it will be stored;
- whether it will be copied;
- how it will be labelled;
- how it will be analysed;
- who will be able to see/listen to the recording;
- how long it will be kept for;
- when and how it will be deleted.

Tip If you want to make your audio recordings available for others to hear (such as oral-history interviews) you must obtain informed consent at the time of the interview (it is much harder to obtain retrospective informed consent). The Oral History Society provides comprehensive guidelines about obtaining informed consent and about the ethical issues involved when obtaining, storing and using oral-history recordings. Visit their website for more information: www.ohs.org.uk/ethics.

Storing Data

As we have seen above, you must make it clear how you intend to store your recordings. However, data storage involves not only keeping your interview recordings, but also storing all your other research data, such as statistics, personal documents, field notes and written transcripts.

Today, most information is stored on digital devices. These can be portable methods (such as memory cards or disks), semi-portable methods (such as hard drives) or inseparable methods (where memory is lost if disconnected from the unit). University researchers should have access to a wide variety of data storage equipment, and IT technicians will be able to offer advice about using the equipment.

All researchers who are storing identifiable data about individuals must comply with data protection legislation (see 'Knowing About Data Protection' below). Also, if you intend to store large and complex data that may be of interest to other researchers and organizations, issues of statistical confidentiality should be incorporated into your methodology (see 'References, Further Reading and Resources' for this chapter at the end of the book).

Knowing About Data Protection

The Data Protection Act 1998 is the main piece of legislation that covers the issue of data protection in the UK. In the European Union the Data Protection Directive covers the protection of individuals with regard to the processing of personal data and the free movement of such data. At this present time, the United States does not have comparable, single legislation concerning data protection. Instead, legislation in the United

States is adopted on an ad hoc basis, combining legislation, regulation and self-regulation.

In the UK the Act relates to all data about living and identifiable individuals that is held, or intended to be held, on computers or in a 'relevant filing system'. These data include contact details, such as telephone numbers, email addresses, names and addresses. They also include identifiable sensitive data such as health, sex life, criminal record, politics, religion, trade union affiliation, ethnicity and race.

However, if your data are anonymous or aggregated (combined from several measurements), this is not regulated by the Act. In these cases extreme care must be taken to ensure that the method you have used to make the data anonymous or aggregated cannot be reversed in any way. More information about anonymity is provided in Chapter 27.

Data protection principles

If you intend to store data about living and identifiable individuals you have to comply with eight important principles of the Act, which state that data must be:

- fairly and lawfully processed;
- processed for limited purposes;
- adequate, relevant and not excessive;
- accurate and up to date;
- not kept for longer than is necessary;
- processed in line with the rights of the individual;
- secure;
- not transferred to other countries without adequate protection.

Tip The Social Research Association (SRA) has produced a publication called *Data Protection Act 1998: Guidelines for Social Research*. It is a useful and detailed publication that covers all the issues relevant to social research, such as data security, disclosure of personal data from research projects and data protection scenarios. A free PDF can be downloaded from the SRA website: www.the-sra.org.uk.

Summary

Knowing how to record and store data is important for all social researchers. The method of recording is influenced by your epistemological and methodological standpoint, and by theoretical perspective. It is also influenced by the topic of your research and the type of people you wish to record. Digital technology has moved on so rapidly that today there are a large number of audio and video devices available for social researchers. Also, electronic storage capabilities have improved significantly, enabling easy and convenient storage but requiring a good understanding of data protection issues.

Another area of technology that has moved on rapidly is the internet. This provides many opportunities for advanced social researchers. These issues are discussed in the following chapter.

17 Using the Internet

The way that you use the internet for your social research depends, in part, on your theoretical perspective and epistemological and methodological standpoint. It can be used as a research tool to distribute questionnaires (in survey research, for example). Or it can be used for unobtrusive research; that is, non-reactive research with 'found' data (perhaps for some type of conversation or discourse analysis, for example).

This chapter illustrates how the internet can be used as a tool for social research, and as a source of data and information for research purposes. It goes on to highlight some of the limitations, problems and pitfalls associated with internet use for social research.

Using the Internet as a Tool for Research

There is a variety of research methods you can use to gather data via the internet. This includes online questionnaires, online focus groups, online interviews, online ethnographies and online experiments.

If you decide to conduct your research online, the advice offered in Stage 3 of this book and the information about sampling offered in Chapter 10 are of particular relevance. Also, you need to bear in mind the limitations of internet research when designing your project (see 'Understanding the

Limitations', below). The books listed in 'References, Further Reading and Resources' for this chapter at the end of the book provide comprehensive information and advice about conducting your research via the internet if these techniques are of interest to you.

Tip Be wary of using online 'survey' services that enable you to construct a questionnaire. Most of these are far too basic; as an advanced researcher you should plan, design and construct your own questionnaire following the advice offered in Chapter 14.

Using the Internet as a Source of Data and Information

You can obtain data and information from the internet in a variety of ways, as described below.

Online journal databases

Universities provide access to online journal databases so that you can search journal abstracts and full-length articles using keywords that match your research topic (and themes that have emerged inductively from your research, for example).

In addition to these subscription databases you can access Google Scholar (http://scholar.google.co.uk), which provides a free way to search for scholarly literature (see Chapter 8). You can search for related works, citations, authors and publications. If the article is not freely available you will be directed to a library or website where the article can be found.

Online repositories

Academic papers, peer-reviewed articles, monographs and book chapters are freely available from online repositories. Details of these repositories can be obtained from the Registry of Open Access Repositories (ROAR), which is hosted by the University of Southampton (http://roar.eprints.org). You can also access scientific and scholarly journals from the Directory of Open Access Journals (www.doaj.org). See Chapter 25 for more information about online repositories and open access publishing.

Datasets

A dataset is a collection of data (gathered by a survey or observation, for example) that is usually presented in tabular form. You can create, manipulate and use existing datasets for your social research project. For example, the Economic and Social Research Council has published details of over 900 datasets generated by ESRC-funded grants. The data are free to access and use. For more information about these datasets, visit www.esrc.ac.uk.

Log files

A log file lists actions that have occurred; for example, web servers maintain log files that list every request made to the server. Log file analysis tools enable you to find out how visitors spend their time on a site, what they look for and the links that they follow. You can use log files to understand social behaviour (website activity can show what people are interested in and what they are searching for on the internet, for example).

Websites

You can visit specific websites for a variety of reasons, such as to gather background information on a research topic, to analyse website text or images or to understand trends and fashion in website design and content.

When using websites to gather background information, it is important to analyse and critique the information using the guidelines provided in Chapter 8. Also, you should record the following (at the time of your visit) if you intend to use any of the information in your thesis/report:

- author's surname and initials (if known);
- date of publication or last revision;
- title of document;
- title of complete work (if relevant);
- URL/web address;
- date of access.

Blogs

Blogs that have been created by academics and students to discuss specific subjects or pieces of research can be very useful to you. Today, there are many leading academics who actively blog and provide trustworthy sources of current opinion and information for researchers. Content is controlled by blog authors and they can decide whether or not to receive comments on their blogs. As a researcher you can read blogs, comment on blogs or write your own blog to gain opinion and feedback on your research.

Podcasts

A podcast is a digital media file (audio or video) that can be downloaded by the target audience. Many are presented as a series and made available as specific episodes over a period of time. Podcasts (especially those presented by eminent researchers) can be useful to you if they cover your topic of research. They can be found on universities' virtual learning environments and on sites such as YouTube.

Wikis

Wikis are simple web pages that students, tutors, researchers and members of the public can create and edit together. The most well-known is Wikipedia (www.wikipedia.org). When wikis are used in research they offer the opportunity for researchers to have equal, active roles as contributors and editors. They are ideal for collaborative research projects. You can use them to find out latest developments in your field and add your personal contributions, based on your research. However, the content of wikis is open to the public and therefore should not contain sensitive material.

Discussion forums

Discussion forums can be a useful source of data for researchers in the areas of health and education, for example. The questions that users ask, the problems that they pose and the advice that is given can all help to inform your project. Also, it is possible to conduct a keyword content analysis of a particular discussion or thread and a thematic analysis of keyword mentions (see Chapter 18).

In cases where users are anonymous, discussions can often be very detailed and frank, perhaps more so than they would be during an interview with a researcher. Although the data are easily accessible and readily available, you should view and analyse with caution (see 'Understanding the Limitations', below).

Social networking sites

Social networking sites can be used by researchers to find, use and disseminate information. They are becoming an increasingly important source of information for market researchers and for researchers who are interested in how people, organizations and governments communicate with each other.

You can observe social behaviour from a distance or become an active participant in networking, for example. If you are interested is using social media as a source of information (and as a research tool) you need to learn and adhere to the rules of each site before engaging.

Micro-blogging sites

Micro-blogging sites provide the potential for researchers to access data immediately after a situation has occurred (the aftermath of a terrorist attack or natural disaster, for example). You can also use micro-blogging sites to communicate ideas and thoughts about your research and the work of others, and to let others know about the main points from conference and seminar papers (if permission has been given), for example.

Tip You can use social media tools to promote your research, increase its visibility, develop new audiences, generate ideas, share the latest information and developments and seek advice and feedback from interested parties.

Photographs and videos

Rapid developments in technology have led to huge increases in the production and transmission of visual forms of communication. Visual data can be both subject matter and a tool of scientific enquiry and the way that this is approached depends on your methodological and epistemological standpoint. For example, you could assess the meaning of visual data found on the internet, or you could analyse the ways in which actors themselves interpret online visual data.

Virtual worlds

Sociologists can use virtual worlds such as 'World of Warcraft' and 'Second Life' to study group formation and social change over time, for example. They provide the opportunity for you to observe behaviour through either participation or non-participation in the virtual world. You can form hypotheses from this observation that can then be applied to the outside world, for example.

Understanding the Limitations

When using the internet for social research purposes you must understand the limitations. These include the following issues:

- Although data are freely available on the internet, they are not necessarily ethically available for research purposes. If possible, permissions should be sought and a careful evaluation undertaken about the consequences of your enquiries on those studied. Steer clear of unwarranted intrusions. Make sure that there will be no undesired and detrimental effects on those studied.

- Not all of the population has access to the internet and some are much more active in their participation than others. You need to be aware that usage can be segregated by demographics such as age, gender, nationality and socio-economic group. Samples need to be designed with these issues in mind and every care should be taken to limit problems with participation bias (see Chapter 10).

- Data are not equally accessible. On social networking sites users can set their own privacy controls. Search engines prioritize data based on complex algorithms. People publishing data may have complex reasons for making sure that some data are in the public domain, while limiting access to other data. Type and level of accessibility must be considered during your project design.

Summary

The internet has the capacity to transform what we, as researchers, know about changes and developments in the social world and about social behaviour. We can use the internet to collect data through questionnaires and focus groups, for example, and we can use the internet as a source of 'found' information that is of relevance to our research topic. When using the internet, however, it is important to be aware of the problems, pitfalls and limitations, as these can influence the success of your project.

This section of the book has offered advice about conducting research and collecting data through a variety of methods. The next section goes on to offer advice about analysing the data that you have collected.

STAGE 4

ANALYSING YOUR DATA

18 Understanding Qualitative Techniques

Qualitative research can generate large amounts of data. There are various ways to analyse these data, and the methods that you choose will depend on your epistemological standpoint, theoretical perspective and your chosen research methodology.

Although issues of validity and reliability are not as strictly laid out as they are in quantitative data analysis, it is still important to make sure that your research is credible, accurate and trustworthy. Careful and systematic analysis (with the aid of software, if relevant) will help you to achieve this. These issues are discussed in this chapter.

Knowing About the Different Qualitative Data Analysis Methods

The more popular methods of qualitative data analysis are listed below, with 'References, Further Reading and Resources' for this chapter provided at the end of the book for those of you who wish to find out more about a particular method. If you are interested in techniques that are not listed here, also see the 'Further Reading' section for comprehensive texts on alternative forms of qualitative data analysis.

Content analysis

Content analysis is used in qualitative research to provide an objective, systematic and quantified description of the data. Using this method the researcher works through textual data, identifying, coding and counting the presence of certain words, phrases, themes, characters or sentences. Data can be in the form of books, interviews, discussions, newspaper headlines or magazine articles, for example.

There are two main types of content analysis: conceptual analysis (a concept is chosen for examination and the number of occurrences recorded) and relational analysis (the relationship between concepts is examined).

There are different ways to approach content analysis, depending on your epistemological and methodological standpoint. For example, coding categories can be generated inductively from the text (naturalistic and contextual) or a relevant theory or research finding can guide the coding (experimental and positivist). Content analysis can be used as the starting point for other types of analysis.

Tip   When undertaking content analysis, you need to consider issues of stability (coders should be able to recode in the same way over a period of time) and reproducibility (a group of coders should be able to classify categories in the same way). You will also need to make sure that your coding is accurate and reliable.

Comparative analysis

Comparative analysis is used to identify, analyse and explain similarities across groups, societies, institutions and cultures. It can be approached in different ways, depending on the type of research and the epistemological and methodological standpoint. For example, the survey method can be used for large-scale international comparisons (in which both qualitative and quantitative analyses can take place), and case studies can be compared and contrasted in a small-scale project (using qualitative techniques), for example.

Specific techniques have been developed for undertaking comparative analysis. For example, Glaser and Strauss (1967) provide guidance about undertaking comparative analysis as part of a grounded theory study, and Ragin (1987) has developed the Qualitative Comparative Analysis (QCA) technique (see 'References, Further Reading and Resources'). Comparative analysis is often used alongside other methods such as thematic and content analysis.

Thematic analysis

Thematic analysis is a popular form of data analysis used in qualitative research. Using this method the researcher works through textual data to identify specific themes (clusters of linked categories that convey similar meanings). To do this, categories are coded, counted, altered and modified in the light of new data. Familiarity with the data is extremely important, so all interviews and transcripts need to be the researcher's own work. Analysis can continue into the writing-up process as themes are modified and tightened.

Thematic analysis is a method favoured by novice researchers because the techniques are easily understood, flexible and are not dependent on a specific epistemology or theoretical perspective. Also, both qualitative and quantitative techniques can be employed (naturalistic and contextual during the inductive process that identifies emergent themes, and experimental and positivist during the deductive process that verifies themes, for example). Thematic analysis can be used as a starting point for other types of analysis.

Discourse analysis

Discourse analysis is a general term that is used to describe a number of different approaches to studying and analysing the uses of language. This can be written, vocal or sign language, for example. Different approaches include semiotics (focusing on how signs and symbols create meaning), deconstruction (exposing contradictions and binary opposites in texts through taking apart the structure of language) and narrative analysis (focusing on how people construct and use stories to interpret the world).

Discourse analysis techniques have been adopted by social constructionists to help them understand social interactions and underlying social structures. Analyses can focus on a variety of issues, such as power relationships in society, the relationship between discourse and interaction, or the relations between text and context, for example. The aim is to identify shared patterns of talking, understand how people construct their own version of events and understand how they use discourse to construct their own identity.

Conversation analysis

Conversation analysis is the study of social interaction within conversation. It is a method used by ethnomethodologists who are interested in finding out how people construct, prolong and maintain their realities. Therefore, the focus is on the construction of reality, rather than the discovery of reality. It differs from discourse analysis because it focuses on the processes of social interaction, rather than discourses (sociocultural phenomena on a larger scale, in the Foucauldian sense).

Researchers are interested in understanding how participants interact with each other, how they contribute during interactions and how they make sense of the contributions that others make during the interaction. Using this method, conversations are collected with little input from the researcher (for example, a video or audio recording is taken when a conversation takes place). Conversations can include interviews, court hearings, telephone calls and classroom discussions, for example. A detailed transcript is produced and analysed to find recurring patterns of interaction.

Using Qualitative Data Analysis Software

Software can be used to analyse texts and media files. It can help with the sorting, structuring and analysing of large amounts of text, but will not provide interpretations. Some data analysis software is easy-to-use, free and open source. Other software is freely available from universities (IT staff will offer advice and guidance on its use).

Most software will now support the different types of analyses that stem from different methodologies, such as content analysis and some types of discourse analysis. Software works through text systematically, assigning codes to major themes and attaching memos to references, ideas and other relevant information. The software will also contain linking, mapping and networking tools.

Tip Using software can save a great deal of time and enable you to handle large volumes of data. It can also help with issues of reliability (see 'Judging the Reliability of Qualitative Analyses', below). However, software may not be suitable for certain types of data analysis and care must be taken to avoid over-reliance on deterministic and rigid processes, rather than on depth, meaning and interpretation.

Judging the Reliability of Qualitative Analyses

There are various criteria used for judging the reliability of qualitative analyses. These vary depending on your epistemological and methodological standpoint and can include the following:

- Credibility: are the results credible and believable from the perspective of the participants in your research? Have the participants had a chance to see the results and do they agree with your findings?

- Sensitivity to context: do your interpretations take the context into account? Are you, as the researcher, attuned to the social context?

- Coherence: are your methods, interpretations and conclusions appropriate to your theoretical perspective and epistemological and methodological stance?

- Rigour: are your interpretations rigorous and accurate? Have you continued with your analyses until your theory is complete?

- Dependability: as the researcher, are you able to account for the ever-changing circumstances in which research occurs? Can you depend on your research to do this?

- Persuasiveness: are your claims established convincingly and backed up with evidence?

- Authenticity: is the research real, genuine and of indisputable origin?

- Trustworthiness: can you, as the researcher, trust your results? Can your participants and other researchers trust the results?

- Confirmation: can your results be confirmed or corroborated? Have your methods been well described and can they be followed by other researchers?

- Transferability: is it possible to transfer the results to other settings or contexts?

- Generalizability: this does not refer to statistical generalization, but instead refers to theoretical generalization. Does your theory provide insights that may be useful in similar contexts?

- Impact and importance: what is the impact of your research? How important are the findings? Have you made these issues clear?

Summary

There are many ways to analyse qualitative data, and the method(s) that you choose depends on your epistemological and methodological standpoint. Data analysis can use an inductive method, a deductive method or a combination of both. Some methods (such as counting and coding in content analysis) follow the rules of quantitative techniques, whereas other methods (such as certain types of discourse analysis) are individual and intuitive. Software can help with the manual process of data analysis but will not provide interpretations.

In qualitative data analysis there are ways to improve the reliability of your research and these, again, depend on your epistemological and methodological standpoint. Quantitative research, on the other hand, has very strict tests for validity and reliability. These issues are discussed in the following chapter.

19 Understanding Quantitative Techniques

All researchers who are intending to undertake a quantitative study will need a basic understanding of statistical techniques. These are described in this chapter along with information about using statistical software and ensuring validity and reliability. This advice is suitable for qualitative researchers who are hoping to undertake a small amount of quantitative analysis and researchers who are new to statistical analysis techniques.

However, if you are an advanced researcher intending to undertake a major quantitative study you will need to move beyond this basic understanding and come to terms with complex statistical analysis techniques. If this is the case, see 'References, Further Reading and Resources' for this chapter at the end of the book.

Tip The conclusions drawn from quantitative data analysis will have little value if you have not addressed your sampling issues appropriately. Refer back to Chapter 10 and read some of the books listed in 'References, Further Reading and Resources' to ensure that you are familiar with sampling techniques. Close attention to sampling methods will provide greater validity to your research conclusions.

Making Use of Statistics

Statistical procedures can be divided into two main categories:

1. *Descriptive statistics*: these are used to describe the population that is under study. They include measures of central tendencies (such as averages: see 'Understanding averages', below) and measures of the variability about the average. This can include range (a measure of the spread of the data between the largest and smallest values) and standard deviation (the variation from the average). These statistics are only used to describe: they are not used to generalize.

2. *Inferential statistics*: these statistics are used by researchers to analyse samples and draw conclusions. They help deductions to be made from the data collected and enable the researcher to test hypotheses and relate findings to the sample or population. Tests of significance are used to address issues of generalizability. (More information about developing hypotheses and related theory is provided in Chapter 21.)

Producing descriptive statistics

If descriptive statistics are your goal all you need to do is count your responses and reproduce them. This is called a *frequency count* or *univariate analysis*. This type of frequency count is usually the first step in any analysis of a large-scale survey and forms the base for many other statistical techniques.

If you are interested in finding out the connections between two variables you will undertake *bivariate analysis* and if you are interested in exploring the connections among more than two variables you will undertake *multivariate analysis.*

Understanding averages

If you want to find a simple average of your data you add up the values and divide by the number of items. This is called an *arithmetic mean.* This is a straightforward calculation used where specific figures can be added together and then divided.

However, it is possible to mislead with averages, especially when the range of the values may be great or there are extreme examples. Researchers, therefore, also describe the *mode* (the most frequently occurring value in the data) and the *median* (the middle value of the range). The mode is calculated by finding the number that occurs most often and the median is calculated by putting the values into order and then finding the middle value.

Using means, modes and medians

The mean is used in *interval scales* when the data are not skewed by extreme values. Interval scales come in the form of numbers with precisely defined intervals and precise comparisons can be made. Examples include answers from questions about age, height and number of children.

The mode is used when dealing with *nominal scales.* In this type of scale the categories include everyone in the sample; no one should fit into more than one category and the implication is that no one category is better than another. Examples of this type of scale include religious preference, race and gender.

The median is used in interval scales (when data are skewed) and in *ordinal scales*. For ordinal scales answers can be placed on a continuum, with the implication being that some categories are better than others. In this type of scale it is not possible to measure the difference between the specific categories. An example of this type of scale is the occupationally based social scale that runs from professional to unskilled manual.

Converting to percentages

Conducting the types of calculations described above can be problematic when there are data missing (for example, some people may not want to answer a question about age or household income). It is possible to overcome the problem of missing data by converting frequency counts to percentages, which are calculated after excluding missing data. However, percentages can be misleading if the total number of respondents is fewer than forty.

Tip If you want to know more about percentages and how they are calculated and used, you may find it useful to work your way through the 'Ratio, Proportion and Percentages' unit, available free of charge from the Open University free resources website (http://openlearn.open.ac.uk).

Using Data Analysis Software

If you have computing software available you should find that this is the easiest and quickest way to analyse your data. Statistical Package for Social Science (SPSS) is the most popular software that is used for social research. The software enables you to undertake complex analyses, produce descriptive statistics, produce charts and tables, and plot distributions and trends.

Most universities run statistics and data analysis courses and/or IT services will provide information leaflets and training sessions on data analysis software. Speak to your supervisor or work colleagues to find out what is available.

Tip If you are new to SPSS you might find it useful to work your way through the 'Getting Started with SPSS' unit, available free of charge from the Open University free resources website (http://openlearn. open.ac.uk). This unit takes a step-by-step approach to statistics software through seven interactive activities, and you don't need statistics software to complete the unit.

Ensuring Validity and Reliability

All scientific research must stand up to rigorous questioning and scepticism. You can help to achieve this by paying close attention to issues of validity and reliability.

Validity

Validity refers to the accuracy of the measurement, asking whether your tests are measuring what they are supposed to measure. There are different types of validity in quantitative research:

■ *Face validity*: are the questions you are using a reasonable way to obtain the information required? Do they appear to be right?

- *Content validity*: do the questions reflect the subject of your research, are all issues included and has anything been left out?

- *Construct validity*: does your test/scale assess the theoretical concept that you say it does?

- *Internal validity*: do your questions really explain the outcome you want to research? Do you have confidence in the cause-and-effect relationship in your study?

- *External validity*: is it possible to generalize to the target population that your survey sample purports to represent?

- *Predictive validity*: does your research have the ability to predict something it should theoretically be able to predict?

- *Concurrent validity*: is your research able to distinguish between groups it should theoretically be able to make a distinction between?

- *Convergent validity*: has your research produced similar results to (converged on) other research that should be theoretically similar?

Reliability

Reliability refers to the way that the research instrument is able to yield the same results in repeated trials. It refers to consistency of measurement and asks whether other researchers would get the same results under the same conditions. Replication of statistically significant results is essential if the scientific community is to accept your hypothesis and establish it as scientific truth.

There are different ways that you can determine the reliability of your measurements:

- *Test-retest reliability*: this assesses the consistency of a measure from one time to another. The same test is given to the same people over a period of time.

- *Parallel form reliability*: this assesses the results of two tests that have been constructed in the same way from the same content domain.

- *Alternative form reliability*: this method uses two tests with the same people, but the same test is not given each time (so that the respondent's memory does not influence the data collected).

- *Inter-observer reliability*: this is used to show how different observers give consistent estimates of the same phenomena.

- *Internal consistency reliability*: this is used to assess the consistency of results across items within a test.

- *Split halves reliability*: this test divides the total number of items into halves and a correlation is taken between the two halves.

See 'References, Further Reading and Resources' at the end of the book to obtain comprehensive information about how to undertake these tests for validity and reliability.

Summary

Quantitative data analysis is the process of presenting and interpreting numerical data and involves the use of descriptive and inferential statistics. Researchers need to know how to calculate the mean, mode and median, and understand the difference between interval, nominal and ordinal scales. Statistical software produced for social researchers is available to help with analysing large amounts of data. Issues of validity and reliability are of great importance if your work is to be taken seriously by the scientific community.

An important part of quantitative data analysis (and qualitative data analysis) is to be able to understand, interpret and critique data. These issues are discussed in the following chapter.

20 Interpreting and Critiquing Data

As an advanced social researcher you will need to spend a considerable amount of time interpreting and critiquing data, research reports and research papers (that have been produced by yourself and by other researchers).

To do this you need to know how to identify and use statistics, facts, opinions and arguments; know how to critique research papers and reports (stemming from qualitative and quantitative methodologies); and learn how to recognize bias. These issues are discussed in this chapter.

Tip To be able to critique research well you need to have a thorough understanding of the research process and research methods. The more you read, the more you will understand. Also, your ability to critique will improve with experience.

Knowing About Statistics, Facts, Opinions and Arguments

When you are interpreting and critiquing data it is important to recognize, and know how to use correctly, statistics, facts, opinions and arguments. This (along with the information provided in Chapters 18 and 19) will help you to make judgements about the validity and reliability of your own work and the work of other researchers.

- Statistics are only as good as the methods used to create them and the skill of the statistician/researcher who collects the data. Figures can be misleading, incorrect (whether deliberate or by mistake) and open to misinterpretation. All statistics (generated by yourself and others) should be analysed carefully before they form part of your research.

- Although, from an objectivist point of view, facts can be investigated and are found to be true, not everything presented as a fact is correct and true. Check your sources and make sure that the information is valid and reliable before presenting facts in your report or believing facts presented in other reports. Your use of (and belief in) facts will depend on your epistemology and theoretical perspective (see Chapter 1).

- Opinions are personal beliefs or judgements that are not based on proof or certainty. Use of opinions in your work will depend on your methodology (and epistemology). All researchers should signpost opinions if they are used in their work. Ensure that you don't mistake opinions for arguments and be wary of opinions disguised as arguments in the work of others.

- Arguments are a coherent set of statements, dialogue or text that is presented to support or reject a view. All arguments used in academic reports must be backed up by evidence. Weak arguments are those that are not backed up adequately or those that focus only on supporting evidence. If you use any arguments that have been made by others, you must acknowledge and reference correctly to avoid plagiarism (see 'Tip', below).

Tip Check that the use of all sources has been acknowledged (in your work and the work of others). Sources can be used for direct citation (where a quote is used, word-for-word or where visual data are reproduced without alteration, for example). They can also be used for indirect citation (where the ideas of another person are reworded or summarized; where facts or data are used that are not common knowledge; or where source material is slightly altered but the main argument remains, for example).

Critiquing Research Reports and Papers

There are different ways to critique existing research reports and papers, and these depend, in part, on whether you are critiquing quantitative or qualitative research. (For more information about evaluating all types of background information, see Chapter 8.)

Critiquing quantitative research

The following points will help you to critique quantitative research (remember to take note of these issues for research reports and papers that you produce yourself, if relevant):

1. Who is the author and what are their credentials? What reason have they for making sure that their information is available?

2. Has the research topic and purpose of the research been well justified?

3. Has the researcher provided a detailed description of the quantitative methodology? Is it clear why this methodology was chosen and how it is the best way to answer the research question?

4. Have the correct procedures been followed when forming hypotheses, generating samples, conducting experiments, analysing data and reaching conclusions? Are the methods well documented?

5. Are the measurements consistent (through repetition and retesting: see Chapter 19)?

6. Have all data been reported (including those that weaken or contradict the results presented)?

7. Is the source you are looking at the original source of the data?

8. Have the data been interpreted correctly? Common mistakes include confusing correlation with causation and ignoring the margin of error.

9. Have the conclusions been scrutinized, tested and verified by other scientists? If not, would it be possible for others to do so?

10. Are the assumptions and conclusions valid and backed up by evidence?

11. Have generalizations been made that are not based on careful experimentation and analysis?

12. Has bias been introduced into any of the information presented (see 'Recognizing Bias', below)? This could be during the hypothesis-forming stage, the experimentation stage, the data collection and analysis stage or when making conclusions and writing up results.

13. Is there a comprehensive literature review and have all other researchers/arguments been well referenced?

14. Is the report well written and presented, following the established rules for scientific reports, with all diagrams, charts, figures and graphs well presented, complete and referenced in the text?

15. Has the importance/impact of the research been demonstrated?

Tip Make sure that statistics apply to the point/argument that is being made. Check that the data has not been manipulated to fit the argument. Visual data should be presented in a way that enables researchers to draw their own conclusions and verify the assertions that have been made.

Critiquing qualitative research

The following questions will help you to critique qualitative research (again, these issues are important for your own research reports and papers, if relevant):

1. Who is the author and what are their credentials? What reason have they for making sure that their information is available?

2. Have the research topic and purpose of the research been well justified?

3. Has the researcher provided a detailed description of the qualitative methodology? Is it clear why this methodology was chosen and how it is the best way to answer the research question?

4. Has a conceptual or theoretical framework been described? Is it adequate and appropriate?

5. Has a philosophical/epistemological discussion been included? Is it adequate and appropriate?

6. Have the research methods been well described? Is there a description of sampling procedures, the method(s) of data collection and the method(s) of data analysis? Are these methods and descriptions appropriate and adequate?

7. Have ethical considerations been taken into account and been well described? Are they adequate and appropriate?

8. Are the results credible, dependable, authentic and trustworthy?

9. Are the results rigorous and accurate? Can the researcher demonstrate that saturation has been achieved (that is, no new results will emerge from the data analysis)?

10. Has a comprehensive literature review been undertaken (if relevant), and have all sources been acknowledged and are they well referenced?

11. Have the findings been presented well? Have they been placed in context? Have they been related to other work on this research topic?

12. Has the importance/impact of the research been demonstrated?

Tip Some researchers find it useful to produce a spreadsheet that can be filled in for every piece of research that they critique. If this method works for you, the columns can include issues such as author, date, publication, research question, methodology (and epistemology/theoretical perspective, if relevant), sample, data collection tools/methods, analysis, findings, strengths, limitations, your opinions/conclusions, relevance to your own research.

Recognizing Bias

'Bias' is a term that is used to describe a tendency or a preference for a particular line of thought, idea, perspective or result. 'Research(er) bias' (or experimenter bias) is used to describe a problem with how the research has been chosen, conducted, analysed and/or reported.

The extent to which bias is seen to be introduced into the research process depends on the epistemological and methodological standpoint and theoretical perspective. For example, researchers approaching their work from the objectivist standpoint will follow set rules and procedures to get rid of bias in the research process (eliminate bias). On the other hand, a researcher approaching from the constructionist standpoint will recognize, define and discuss the types of bias that could be introduced (acknowledge bias), believing that it is impossible to eliminate bias completely.

It is important to recognize bias in your work and the work, thoughts, ideas and research of others. This is the case for both objective and subjective work: both can involve bias (even if the scientific method is used), and through careful interpretation, critique and analysis (following the procedures outlined above) you should be able to recognize when this occurs. Exercise 8 will also help you to become more aware of bias.

Exercise 8: Critiquing and Recognizing Bias

As you work through your critiques of other research reports and papers, keep a record of all types of bias that you can identify. This can include researcher bias (e.g. the selection of data that stand out to the researcher), reactivity bias (e.g. the influence the researcher has on the participants), selection bias (e.g. the sample is not representative of the population) and measurement bias (e.g. participants do not answer all the questions or they answer in a way they think they should answer).

Refer to your list throughout your own research project so that you can take action to eliminate or acknowledge bias (depending on your epistemological standpoint).

Summary

All advanced social researchers need to understand how to interpret and critique their work and the work of other researchers. This will help you to ensure that statistics, facts, opinions and arguments are used correctly, enable you to judge the validity and reliability of research reports and papers, and help you to recognize when and how bias has been introduced into the research process.

Another important part of the research process for advanced researchers is to develop theory. This can follow a deductive or an inductive process (or a combination of both), depending on epistemology and methodology. These issues are discussed in the following chapter.

21 Developing Theory

A theory is a coherent group of general propositions (or a set of principles or statements) used as an explanation of a class of phenomena on which action can be based. Theories are analytical tools that help researchers understand, explain and make predictions about a given subject matter. Researchers can work top-down (grand theory to local) or bottom-up from the data.

For researchers from the objectivist standpoint, theory is the most scientific, reliable, rigorous and comprehensive form of knowledge, which has been generated using the scientific method. For researchers from the constructionist and subjectivist standpoints, theories provide complex and comprehensive conceptual understandings of the social world, interactions and behaviour, and have been generated from observation and analysis. These two approaches to developing theory are discussed in this chapter.

Generating Theory Deductively and Inductively

The two main approaches to generating theory (deductive and inductive) depend on epistemology, theoretical perspective and methodology, as described below.

Deductive theory generation

Researchers approaching their work from an objectivist stand-point use a deductive method of theory generation, which involves putting forward a hypothesis for testing. In the traditional science view, a hypothesis is an idea about a phenomenon or observation that is tentative and not proven. However, once it has been tested repeatedly and the probability of error has been greatly reduced, the hypothesis can be developed into a theory.

For a theory to stand up to scientific scrutiny, evidence for its development must be shown clearly and it must be able to explain existing phenomena and make predictions about the future (see Chapters 19 and 20).

For deductive theory generation there are six main stages to work through:

1. ask questions in the form of a hypothesis;
2. look for patterns to support or disprove your hypothesis (gather background information and observe);
3. formulate your theory, based on the hypothesis;
4. design experiments to test your theory;
5. analyse data, draw conclusions and further develop your theory;
6. report your results and make them available for scrutiny (full disclosure).

Close attention must be paid to issues of reliability and validity throughout your research (complex techniques are available to help with this process: see Chapter 19).

Tip Theory generation is a long and laborious process. Short cuts cannot be taken. False turns can lead the theory off course, so care must be taken to avoid (and acknowledge) these false turns and action taken to get back on course.

Inductive theory generation

Researchers approaching their work from a constructionist or a subjectivist standpoint tend to use an inductive method of theory generation, although they can also work through a process of deductive theory generation (depending on methodology). In inductive theory generation observation leads to the discovery, or recognition, of certain patterns, themes, categories, world views or empirical generalizations that are then explored further, with the ultimate aim of generating theory.

Procedures for inductive theory generation vary depending on the methodological standpoint. As a general guide you may need to work through the following stages:

1. begin your enquiry by observing a phenomenon or behaviour;
2. develop your research questions based on these observations (and existing literature, if relevant);
3. answer these questions through more in-depth observation or questioning;
4. develop your theory, based on these in-depth observations and analysis;
5. test and modify your theory with further observation and analysis (or through deductive methods);
6. report your results (tightening and modifying as you write).

Although there are no set procedures for ensuring validity and reliability in qualitative research, it is important to ensure that your theory has been developed from credible, authentic, dependable and trustworthy research (see Chapter 18).

Techniques to Help with Inductive Theory Generation

- Become very familiar with your data. Be very observant.

- Look for anything unusual or that stands out. Try to explain why this might be.

- Categorize into types. Search for common denominators and differences between and within types.

- Consider extreme cases. This can include searching for cases that are totally different, or reversing your thinking, for example.

- Compare and contrast cases. Look for similar and contrasting events and phenomena in your own research and in existing work.

- Use diagrams and pictures to help you to see connections between themes, categories and types.

- Recognize themes that exist in different topics. Begin to note the importance of themes that repeat themselves.

- Mix and muddle categories, themes, types and cases (manually or digitally). Rearrange to form connections.

- Build analytical categories that can be integrated into a developing theoretical scheme or framework.

■ Share, discuss and build on your ideas with other researchers/colleagues. Cross disciplinary boundaries to expand and strengthen themes, concepts and theory.

■ Express your basic concept in one sentence: the process of writing can challenge the precision of your conceptualizations.

Reasoning Deductively and Inductively

Both procedures described above involve the ability to 'reason'; that is, the ability to think analytically about an issue and arrive at a conclusion or opinion that will help to develop theory.

Deductive reasoning is a process of arriving at a conclusion based on previously known facts. It can only be sound if the premise on which it is based is true. When producing your own work (and evaluating the work of others), you need to know, and make clear, the premise on which deductive reasoning is based, check that it is true and work through the reasoning to make sure that the conclusion is valid (see Chapter 20). Through doing this you will help to increase the external validity of your work and help to ensure that you can make generalizations to the target population that your survey sample purports to represent.

Inductive reasoning involves a process of arriving at a conclusion based on observation. The conclusions drawn must be real, genuine and of indisputable origin. They must be established convincingly and backed up with evidence (see Chapter 18). This will help to ensure that your developing theory provides insights that will be useful in similar contexts.

Exercise 9: Recognizing Problems with Reasoning

It is important to note that both inductive and deductive reasoning can go wrong. Recognize and note down when this occurs in other research projects. An awareness of the problems that can occur will help you to think more about the development of your own thoughts, hypotheses and theories.

Generating Successful Theory

For your theory to be successful it should meet the following criteria:

- Successful theories are plausible, feasible, testable, predictable and verifiable. They are short, well described and easily understood.

- Successful theories are those that connect information from different and disparate areas and bring out the relationships between them.

- Successful theories are valid as long as there is no evidence to dispute them. However, good theories can invite disagreement, alternatives and better explanations.

- Successful theories can be modified and adapted.

- Successful theories are general, parsimonious and falsifiable (that is, no theory can ever be considered certain). The longer a theory stands without falsification of its core principles, the stronger it becomes.

Tip New and important theoretical insights can come at any time (especially during the night). Always carry equipment with you to record your thoughts and ideas wherever you are.

Summary

Theory can be generated using deductive and inductive methods, and the method that is used depends on the epistemological and methodological standpoint. Some researchers use a combination of both methods in their research project, if their methodological framework allows for this. Theory generation can be a long and laborious process, but it is an essential component of advanced-level research. Theories must be plausible, predictable and verifiable and stand up to scientific scrutiny.

This section of the book has provided information about analysing data and developing associated theory. The next section will move on to provide information about the various methods that can be used to report and share your research results.

STAGE 5

REPORTING YOUR RESULTS

22 Producing Your Thesis

If you are a postgraduate student (at Master's or doctoral level) you will need to produce a thesis that is submitted in support of your candidature for an academic degree. The style, structure and length of theses vary, depending on academic level, subject area and individual university rules and regulations. However, there are basic rules that you should follow when producing your thesis, and advice and guidance about these issues are provided in this chapter.

Tip Before you start to write your thesis you may find it useful to write some journal papers with an experienced researcher, such as your supervisor (see Chapter 24). This will help you to become familiar with academic writing and will provide useful information for inclusion in your thesis (perhaps as an appendix, if relevant).

Writing Your Thesis

In most cases writing is to do with presenting your results, rather than finding new results. However, for some researchers approaching their work from constructionist or subjectivist standpoints, writing can be useful to help develop theory, organize concepts, reveal possible problem areas and provide new insights.

In cases such as these you might find it useful to begin the writing process at an earlier stage than researchers who approach their work from an objectivist standpoint (writing occurs only when all experiments are completed and conclusions are reached).

When writing your thesis you should take note of the following:

- Your thesis must be written at the right level. Although your writing must be clear and precise, you must display technical and expert knowledge. When technical terms are used, make sure that you understand exactly what they mean.

- Avoid informalities, conversational language, generalizations and opinions (unless they fit with your methodology). Ensure that your style is in keeping with international standards of a doctoral or Master's education.

- Never make sweeping generalizations such as 'academics state' or 'scholars suggest'. Always be specific with references, giving exact names and dates.

- In some cases bullet points or a series of numbered points may provide the best way to explain a finding. However, use these techniques sparingly: your thesis should provide a connected and convincing argument, rather than a list of observations and facts.

- Make sure that your original contribution to knowledge is highlighted and well signposted for examiners.

- Check for spelling mistakes, grammatical errors and typing mistakes. Although examiners might not fail you for these, it will cast doubt in their minds.

Tip Universities recognize the importance of producing graduates who can communicate sophisticated information to sophisticated audiences. Therefore, many now provide additional training and support in the form of writing workshops, individual writing consultations and non-credit writing courses. Ask your supervisor for more information about what is available at your university.

Structuring Your Thesis

In general, your thesis should include the following sections:

1. a title page to include the officially approved thesis title, your name, the name of your university, the degree for which the thesis is submitted and the date of submission (the title must correspond exactly to the title on the thesis submission form or exam entry form);

2. an abstract that summarizes context, methods, results and conclusions (your original contribution to knowledge should be made clear);

3. acknowledgements;

4. a table of contents to include chapter headings (numbered sequentially), subheadings and page numbers;

5. a list of figures, diagrams, graphs, etc. (if relevant);

6. an introduction that provides a justification for your research and lists your aims and objectives;

7. a critical assessment of related literature and research;

8. a detailed description of, and justification for, your chosen methodology and theoretical perspective (including relevant theoretical and methodological literature);

9. a detailed description of, and justification for, your chosen research methods (in a way that your methods can be reproduced, if relevant);

10. a detailed account of your results and conclusions;

11. your theory (and original contribution to knowledge);

12. a discussion on how your results and theory relate to other research in the field, the relevance and impact of your findings and information about how the research and theory could be advanced or continued;

13. detailed references and bibliography;

14. appendices to include relevant information that helps the reader to understand your work further (relevant journal or conference papers, interview transcripts, questionnaires or diagrams/graphs that are relevant, but haven't been referred to specifically in the text, for example).

Submitting Your Thesis

Rules and regulations about thesis submission vary considerably. Most universities require you to submit one hard-bound copy for their library stock and two soft-bound copies for external examiners. They have strict rules about page layout, font, binding colour and lettering on the binding. Your university binding service and supervisor will provide further advice.

Some universities now require a thesis to be submitted in electronic form and will provide information and guidance about how to do this and the format that it should take. For hard copies you will need to pay a binding fee and for electronic copies you will need to pay a processing fee.

Make sure that you obtain information about submission rules and procedures as soon as you start to write your thesis so that you can produce it in the correct format from the outset. This is of particular importance if your university requires electronic copies as you will need to meet the technical and production requirements and make sure that you adhere to any file-naming conventions. Some universities provide templates to make electronic submission easier for their students.

Tip Make sure that you produce a personal copy of your thesis (this only requires a soft binding) so that you can take it to your viva. This can be a proofread version on which small corrections have been made if you want to save money on additional printing and binding.

Understanding the Examination Process

PhD theses are examined by a group of examiners (or an exam committee). In many universities it is accepted practice to choose your own examiners. In general, you will need to choose one external examiner and up to three internal examiners, one of which can be your supervisor. As an expert in your field you will be familiar with other experts in your field. Take note of these early on in your research and begin to think about who would make a good examiner. It is important to choose someone who is both familiar with your topic and with your research methodology and methods. Steer clear of examiners who might approach your topic from a very different epistemological and methodological standpoint as they may find it hard to agree with, and understand, how you have approached your research.

Try to meet with potential examiners at conferences and seminars. Discuss your research with them to find out what they think about your work. Read papers that have been produced by potential examiners to gain more of an insight into their ideas, thoughts and previous research. Discuss your thoughts about potential examiners with your supervisor and ask for suggestions if you are struggling to find suitable candidates.

Producing a Successful Thesis

You will enhance your chances of success if you take note of the following points when producing your thesis:

- Your thesis must be your own account of your research.

- Your work must be original and point to the discovery of new facts, ideas or theory and provide a demonstration of independent, critical thought.

- Your thesis should demonstrate your ability to carry out independent research and present your work in a coherent document.

- Your thesis must be of publishable quality (well presented, well written, well argued and produced in the correct format).

- Any collaborated work must be acknowledged and certified by your supervisor.

Tip It is extremely important to build a good, trusting relationship with your supervisor. Make sure that you present draft copies of each chapter when requested, and listen to, and take note of, any feedback and advice offered.

Summary

All postgraduate students need to submit a thesis that is read and examined by both internal and external examiners (for PhD level submissions). The thesis needs to be an original piece of work that clearly demonstrates competence at the required level. Universities have strict rules and procedures about thesis production and submission. These should be understood at an early stage so that the thesis can be produced in the right way. A good working relationship with your supervisor is crucial.

Once a thesis has been submitted and examined, PhD candidates (and some Master's students) are invited to discuss their research and thesis. This is called a viva and is discussed in the next chapter.

23 Passing Your Viva

A viva (or viva voce) is an oral examination that is used to test a student's knowledge and defence of their thesis. It is mostly used at doctoral level, although some undergraduate and Master's students can be called to attend a viva.

The purpose of a viva is to prove that the thesis is your own work, to show that you understand what you have written, to demonstrate an awareness of the wider literature and to show that you understand the importance/impact of your work and how it can be developed further. This chapter gives advice about preparing for and undertaking your viva, completing your viva successfully and understanding viva outcomes.

Preparing for Your Viva

Consider the following points when preparing for your viva:

■ Try to arrange a date for your viva as soon as possible after thesis submission, but leave enough time for your preparation. Note down the time, date and venue as soon as it is arranged. Visit the venue beforehand, if possible, so that you know what to expect.

■ Reread your thesis carefully. Try to detach yourself from your work and produce a critical analysis using the information offered in Chapter 20. Try to anticipate the type of questions that will be asked about each section of your thesis.

- Ask your supervisor/graduate office for sample viva questions and prepare answers for each. Some supervisors will even provide a mock viva if you ask.

- Explain your theory to a lay audience when the opportunity arises. This will help you to simplify your arguments and present them coherently and comprehensibly.

- In Chapter 22 you were advised to keep a spare, bound copy of your thesis to take with you to your viva. Write a few pertinent notes on the contents page and place a few bookmarks in crucial sections. Know the structure of your thesis well so that you can find information easily (use a bound copy as it looks more professional and is easier to read than reams of loose paper).

Tip Memorize a few specific dates, key names, titles and journal articles so that you can mention them during your viva.

Undertaking Your Viva

The duration of a viva varies, depending on the subject of your research, the level of degree, regulations set by your university and the preferences of examiners. In general, however, they tend to last from forty-five minutes to two hours.

Examiners need to assess your strengths and weaknesses. Some do this in a more aggressive way than others. Remain calm and passive: it is important not to take anything personally, but try to answer each question fully, politely and in a non-confrontational way, despite the manner in which it may have been asked. Don't be afraid to discuss the flaws in your work: show that you recognize the problems and illustrate how it would be possible to overcome them and expand on your research.

If you have prepared well for your viva you will be able to show that you are familiar with the structure and content of your thesis. Bookmarks, notes and personal familiarity should help you to find the pertinent sections quickly. Try not to flick through your thesis desperately seeking information that you cannot find.

Completing Your Viva Successfully

The following points will help you to complete your viva successfully:

- Familiarity with your thesis is crucial. In addition to writing your thesis (see Chapter 22) you should take the opportunity to present conference papers (see Chapter 26), seminar papers and write journal articles (see Chapter 24). This will provide experience in presenting, arguing and defending your thesis to an academic audience. It also provides the opportunity to receive feedback from other researchers who may pick up on issues that are deemed important by your examiners. Take note of 'Case Study: Anna', below, and don't make the same mistakes.

- Debating skills are important. If you think these skills need improving, try to strengthen them by practising before your viva. When structuring your speech, think about pros and cons, strengths and weaknesses, definition of terms, the presentation of your argument and the presentation of evidence to back-up your argument.

- Find out all you can about your examiners. Read their publications and become familiar with their work. Speak to them at conferences if the situation arises. Consider their preferred methodology and theoretical perspective. If this differs from yours, try to anticipate questions they might ask about your methodology (or think about the ways that they might critique your methodology).

- Most examiners are interested in the wider impact of your work, so try to take a step back to look at the broader picture. Make sure that you keep up-to-date with what is happening in your field since you completed your thesis (unfortunately, some oral examinations can only be arranged several months after you have submitted your thesis, so you must continue to review the literature and keep on top of current thinking while you are waiting).

Case Study: Anna

At the beginning of my third year I went to a conference to present a paper on my findings so far. My paper was to be presented in a one-hour session with another researcher who had written a paper on a similar topic and the session was to be chaired by another researcher. Well, it turned into a nightmare. The person who was chairing the session was very much into quantitative, survey research. I was at the other end of the spectrum with a highly qualitative piece of work. He didn't even let me finish my paper before he started belittling my methods, in quite an aggressive way. Then he tried to trash my results because my methods weren't sound, in his eyes. I was flabbergasted, as were quite a few people in the room. This is not the role of someone brought in to chair a session.

Anyway, it left me with a really bad taste, so much so that I refused to read any more of his research, nor reference his books and papers in my thesis. Unfortunately, during my viva my external examiner noticed this and asked why I hadn't mentioned his work, as the topic, if not the methods, was so close to mine. I struggled with an answer. I didn't want to appear unprofessional or show that I hadn't read all the relevant literature. In the end I decided to be honest and explain what had happened and luckily the examiners accepted it.

My advice would be to not put yourself in this position. Keep everything at an academic level. I would have been better off reading his work and then writing a critical analysis, rather than leaving it out entirely. Don't let personal dislikes influence your academic work. Keep professional.

Understanding Viva Outcomes

Although procedures vary, in general there are seven possible outcomes from your viva:

1. Your degree is awarded immediately with no need for changes or amendments.
2. Your degree will be awarded, subject to minor amendments, which must be submitted within a stated time (e.g. one month).
3. Your degree will be awarded, subject to larger amendments to be made within a stated time (e.g. six months).
4. Your thesis will need to be revised and resubmitted. This may require substantial rewriting of certain parts of your thesis.
5. In rare cases you may be required to rewrite your thesis and resubmit for a lower degree classification.

6. In rare cases you may be awarded a lower degree with or without minor amendments. If amendments are required they must be made within the stated time.

7. In very rare cases your thesis will be failed with no right to resubmit.

Appealing the decision

Most universities enable you to appeal the outcome of your viva if you are awarded a lower degree classification or if your thesis fails with no right to resubmit. When making your appeal, you will need to provide a detailed explanation of your case, using the official channel. Your supervisor or graduate office will provide further advice about the procedure.

Summary

All doctoral students need to undertake a viva before they can be awarded their degree. Careful preparation and familiarity with your thesis are extremely important, as is experience in defending your theory (both written and oral). Supervisors and graduate offices will be able to offer further advice about specific viva rules and regulations at your university.

Writing journal articles is a useful way to become more familiar with your work as it enables you to structure your thoughts and present them in a clear and coherent way. It is also a useful way to disseminate your ideas and obtain feedback from other researchers, which will help you to refine and expand your ideas and successfully pass your viva. Information about writing journal articles is provided in the next chapter.

24 Writing Journal Articles

Writing journal articles is an important part of being an advanced researcher. This is especially so for researchers who intend to make a career out of academia. Producing academic articles enables you to develop your ideas, describe your emerging techniques, challenge widely held views, disseminate results and improve your academic career prospects. It also enables you to advance theory and add to existing knowledge in your field. This chapter provides information about finding suitable journals, producing and submitting articles, knowing about author identification and affiliation when writing, and understanding the article acceptance process.

Finding Suitable Journals

As an advanced researcher you will be familiar with the journals that cover your field of research. You will probably also be familiar with journals that cover your epistemology, methodology and theoretical perspective. Your supervisor will be able to offer further advice about suitable journals. Keep notes of these journals throughout your research project. Try to read articles from these journals regularly so that you can become familiar with the preferred content and style.

Once you have identified a journal that would be suitable for an article, obtain guidelines about house style, content and submission. Make sure that you adhere to these guidelines as most editors are very strict about what will be accepted. For example, some journal editors prefer author identities to be kept in the background (passive, third person), whereas others are happy to let the voice of the author speak (first person with personal intervention: see 'Presenting Identity and Affiliation', below). If you are unsure about whether your article is suitable, contact the editor for advice.

Tip Some journal editors ask that you write a short letter or email about your proposed article before you submit. If this is the case, make sure that you do so. This will stop you wasting valuable time and effort producing an article that won't be accepted.

Producing and Submitting a Journal Article

When producing and submitting a journal article, you should take note of the following:

- If you are new to writing articles for journals you may find it useful to write your first few articles with an experienced academic writer (this will probably be your supervisor(s): see 'Case Study: Bridget', below).

- Consider all the reasons why journal articles are rejected (see 'Reasons Why Journal Articles Are Not Accepted' box, below). Make sure that you don't make any of these mistakes.

- Follow all journal house-style guidelines, making sure that the article is of the correct style and length and that it is pitched at the right level for the journal readers.

- Produce a good title. This should be clear and concise. It should not trivialize your research, nor oversell it. Ambiguous, misleading or unnecessary words should be avoided.

- Write the article and leave it for a while. Return to the draft and edit/proofread as appropriate. Ask experienced colleagues to read the draft and provide honest feedback.

- Ensure that your article is robust, plausible and based on sound and credible methodology.

- Pay close attention to the abstract (or lead). Make sure that it grabs attention and points to your methodology and the original contribution to knowledge. Abstracts are copyright free and can be made available online. Journal editors will be keen for other researchers to read your article, based on your abstract.

- Submit your article when you think it is as good as it can be. Only submit the same article to one journal at a time. Follow all submission guidelines (most now accept email submissions). Make sure that all material (such as images, captions, keywords and the abstract) is included when you submit. Also, you will need to ensure that you have the necessary permissions (to use images, poetry or prose extracts, for example) before you submit.

Reasons Why Journal Articles Are Not Accepted

- The author has not followed journal guidelines about house style, length and content.

- The article content and/or style are not suitable for the journal.

- The article is poorly presented and contains too many errors.

- The research does not add to existing knowledge. The study replicates existing work and does not provide anything new.

- The conceptual framework is badly developed (this could be due to a lack of background reading, for example).

- The methodology is flawed (the methodology is not suited to the research question, for example).

- Methodological detail and information about research methods are lacking. It is unclear how the researcher has obtained the results that are being reported. It is impossible for others to check or verify the results.

- Journal referees are critical of the findings/methods (perhaps due to problems with validity and reliability, for example) and cannot recommend the article for publication: see 'Understanding the Acceptance Procedure' below.

Presenting Identity and Affiliation

Journal articles convey content and carry a representation of the writer. It is not only what you write, but how you write (and the way in which you engage in specialist discourses). Your identity and affiliation can be portrayed through writing. However, for most academic writing you need to select words and ways of writing that influence and persuade, and that have meaning for a particular genre and academic community. You also have to follow journal conventions. Therefore, the identity and affiliation that you present may not be a matter of free choice.

For researchers approaching their work from the objectivist standpoint this is of little consequence. Indeed, journal articles should follow set rules and procedures and the identity and affiliation of the writer should be kept in the background (the positivist assumption that academic research should be objective). In this case impersonality and author invisibility are important (text is written in the third person and personal intervention is avoided).

Researchers approaching their work from a constructionist and subjectivist standpoint, however, argue that identity and affiliation are important and that the writer's life-history (or personal identity) is projected in the text. In these cases the first person can be used, authors are visible and personal intervention can be included.

Case Study: Bridget

One of my supervisors suggested we should collaborate on a journal article. I was interested in the word 'collaborate' as it meant me writing the whole article and him just making a few grammatical changes. It was problematic because I wanted to write in the first person, but he said this was unprofessional so I had to change it all. When it was published his name appeared first. I thought this was a bit much, but apparently it was common practice in that department.

I later wrote another article with my other supervisor and the whole experience was very different. We both wrote sections in the first person and then both critiqued each other's work, refining and amending until we were both happy with the final outcome. Even though we had both done equal amounts of work my supervisor insisted that my name appeared first when the article was published. This may seem a small issue, but I think it is important for citations and for my future research career.

I learnt a lot from both supervisors, but enjoyed the experience much more with the second.

Understanding the Acceptance Procedure

Once you have submitted your article it will be sent for review. Editors can use up to six peer-reviewers (depending on the journal). Many of these are academics who are not paid to review articles, so this process can take longer than you might wish (you can ask for a progress report if decisions are taking too long). Good editors will try to ensure that the process moves quickly and many now use manuscript tracking software to coordinate the flow of high numbers of submissions.

Once your article has been reviewed there tend to be four outcomes:

- accept;
- accept with minor revisions;

- accept with major revisions;
- reject.

The editor will provide a summary of the comments made by the reviewer(s) and you will need to make changes accordingly, if relevant. Changes should be made and returned as soon as possible (some editors will insist that the paper is submitted as a brand-new submission if too much time has elapsed).

If your paper is accepted you will be asked to sign a 'Licence to Publish' or an 'Assignment of Copyright'. You should read this carefully to find out what you can and can't do with your paper when it is published. Your paper will be copyedited and you will be required to proofread the final copy before it is published. For information about publishing online, see Chapter 25.

Summary

Writing journal articles will help you to develop your ideas, disseminate your results and obtain valuable feedback on your research. You will improve your chances of getting published if you make sure that you follow journal guidelines and submissions rules, ensure that your article is written for (and targeted at) the right audience, your methodology is sound (and well described) and you have an original contribution to make to existing knowledge in your field of research.

Many academic journals and universities now publish papers online. It is also possible for you to self-publish your work online through blogs, personal websites and university websites. These issues are discussed in the following chapter.

25 Publishing Online

The internet provides the opportunity for researchers to share their results on a worldwide basis, efficiently and often at no financial cost to themselves. Open access has enabled barriers to be broken down so that any interested reader can now access scholarly journals without having to pay a subscription. Social media and personal/university websites enable researchers to engage in complex scientific discussion and collaborate on interesting projects. This chapter provides information about the open access movement, depositing books in repositories and using personal websites and social media to disseminate results.

Using Open Access Publishing

Open access publishing is gaining momentum, with an increasing number of funding bodies now requiring that grant holders make their work available through open access channels. This is the practice of publishing academic, peer-reviewed articles, monographs and book chapters on the internet with unrestricted access. This increases the visibility of research and opens it up to a worldwide audience. There are two main types of open access publishing:

- Repository-based green open access publishing: the author publishes in a journal and then self-archives an unformatted/pre-print copy in an institutional or sub-ject-based repository (see 'Depositing Papers in Institutional Repositories', below).

■ Gold open access: the author publishes in an open access journal, but the article is only made available on payment of a publication or processing fee. This fee should be paid by the author's institution or funding body (the cost of the fee is included in the grant proposal, for example). However, it is feared that early career researchers, inde-pendent researchers, doctoral students and researchers from developing countries may struggle to pay publication fees under this model.

Tip Open access is different from open content. When journal articles are published through an open access model they are made available on the internet (with unrestricted access) but others cannot modify or change content. The article is attributed to one author or a group of authors. Open content, on the other hand, enables others to modify, edit and change articles that are freely available. This type of article is not attributed to any particular author.

Depositing Papers in Institutional Repositories

Many higher education institutions now require that all articles and conference papers are deposited in their repository (with a voluntary deposit of book chapters and monographs, if pub-lisher permission is sought). Rules and regulations for depositing articles, papers, monographs and chapters in insti-tutional repositories vary, so contact your university repository staff for specific information and guidance.

Most universities enable authors to self-deposit and provide instructions about how to do this. You will need to register with, and log on to, the system, provide basic bibliographic details about your publication and upload the full text (in the required format). Alternatively, you will be able to send your paper to repository members of staff who will be able to deposit your work for you. They will also check that copyright agreements are adhered to, ensure that your publisher allows the paper to be deposited in the repository and, if not, ensure that the full text is not made publicly available.

Tip When submitting a paper to an institutional or subject-based repository it should not be the final (published version) as most publishers will not allow this. Instead, it can be a pre-print version (before peer review and prior to acceptance) or a post-print version (after peer review and acceptance, but not the final draft) (see 'Disseminating Results on Personal Websites' and 'Using Social Media to Disseminate Results', below).

Disseminating Results on Personal Websites

If you have had a paper published in a journal you should check first whether you are able to publish the paper on your own website (rules vary, depending on the publisher). This is a copyright issue and you need to find out whether you transferred copyright to the publisher when your paper was accepted for publication.

In most cases you will be able to publish an earlier version of your paper (this could be an unformatted version of your manuscript that was sent prior to publication, for example). This practice has become widespread due to a loophole in copyright agreements that enables authors to share pre-print versions of their work (some publishers have now closed this loophole).

If you are not permitted to publish under an existing agreement, it is possible to contact your publisher to ask for written permission to publish. Some will grant this, depending on the journal, the topic and the date of publication.

When placing work on your personal website you should also take care to ensure that your work does not contain materials on which the copyright is held by a third party. This can include graphs, images and diagrams, for example. In these cases you will need to obtain the necessary permissions before you publish.

Tip Most publishers will not accept an article for publication that has already been published elsewhere. This can include personal websites. If you hope to get a paper published in a journal, think carefully about whether you should place the final version on your website before you have sent it to a journal editor for acceptance and publication.

Using Social Media to Disseminate Results

In Chapter 17 we saw how social media can be used for research purposes. It can also be used to disseminate research findings. This can be done directly through the publication of draft research papers via personal blogs, for example. This can encourage in-depth conversation and feedback about results. It can also be done indirectly through providing links to papers in open access repositories on micro-blogging or social network sites, for example (and documents, images and graphs can be attached to micro-blogging posts).

When using social media to disseminate your research results, you need to take note of the following:

- Check your online presence on a regular basis (see 'Tip', below). False or misleading information can spread quickly and you need to make sure that this is not attributed to you.

- Make sure that you don't breach copyright issues when publishing through social media. If a journal has published your paper previously you need to check whether you are able to publish an unformatted version online.

- Comments can be anonymous. It is easy for others to be derogatory and even insulting about your work. Don't enter into bitter arguments: keep everything on a professional, academic level (intellectual analysis and critique should be taken on board while personal insults should be ignored).

Tip As a researcher you should check your online presence on a regular basis to make sure that you are not being incorrectly credited with work that could damage your scholarly reputation. You should also sign up for an Open Researcher and Contributor Identifier (Orcid). This is a unique code that is assigned to each researcher, making it easier for electronic databases to identify authors accurately. For more information and to sign up, visit http://about.orcid.org.

Summary

Recent technological developments have led to a rapid rise in the use of the internet to disseminate research findings. This can be done by depositing papers in university or funding-body repositories, through open access journals and through personal websites, blogs and social media sites. Your work reaches a much wider audience and can attract comments and critiques from all over the world. When using the internet it is important to act professionally and monitor your online presence for problems and abuse.

Conference papers can also be placed on personal websites and in institutional repositories, if the copyright agreement allows it. As an advanced social researcher you will find it useful to present your findings at conferences as this is another way to share your ideas and obtain feedback from other researchers. These issues are discussed in the next chapter.

26 Presenting at Conferences

Writing and presenting conference papers is an important activity for all advanced researchers. It enables you to share your research findings with other researchers, receive feedback, generate ideas, develop your thoughts for your thesis and improves your academic career prospects. It also enables you to attend other presentations and find out what other researchers are doing in your field.

When presenting a paper you need to find the right conference, succeed in getting your abstract accepted, prepare appropriately and present your paper, using relevant visual aids and/or presentation software. These issues are discussed in this chapter.

Finding a Suitable Conference

As an advanced researcher you should be familiar with organizations that arrange conferences in your field. Subscribe to all relevant mailing lists so that you can find out about conferences as soon as they are announced. The following points will help you to find a suitable conference:

- If you are new to presenting at conferences, and you are at an early stage of your career, you might have more chance of acceptance if you submit to a small local or regional conference, rather than a larger, national conference.

- Find out as much as you can about conference attendees. How many people will attend? Who are they, where do they come from and what are their areas of expertise? Will meeting these people and listening to their papers help with your own research?

- Find out as much as you can about the structure of the conference. How are papers presented (to a full audience, in workshops or in a panel discussion, for example)? Do presenters read their papers or present their ideas as a discussion topic? Are you happy to present your paper in this way?

Tip Some organizations will specify that you have to be a member before you can present a paper at their conference, so find out whether or not this is the case. Your department may have a group membership, or you may be able to join and have your subscription fee reimbursed by your department.

Submitting an Abstract

Once you have found a suitable conference, in most cases, you will need to submit an abstract. This should be clear and concise and should give information about your topic, your methods and your original contribution to knowledge. It should demonstrate clearly that your paper will be relevant to the topic of the conference, relevant to the audience and pitched at the right level (using the right terminology). Make sure that you submit your abstract within the required deadline and in the correct format.

At this stage it is important to understand what sort of paper is required so that you can plan accordingly. For example, if you are the only person to present a paper in a one-hour session, you will need a much longer and more detailed paper than you would need for a panel session where you are presenting with other researchers. Make sure that you obtain this information before you submit the abstract.

Preparing Your Paper

The following points will help you to prepare your conference paper:

■ Write your paper, making sure that it follows the criteria set by the conference organizers in terms of length, structure and style (if relevant). Grab attention quickly. Pay close attention to grammar, spelling and punctuation. Keep focused on your theme. Take care not to insult the intelligence of your audience but don't assume that everyone is an expert. If you are writing for a scientific audience, see 'References, Further Reading and Resources' for this chapter at the end of the book.

■ Once you have written your paper, rewrite it for an oral presentation. This involves the inclusion of oral clues, such as making transitions in your argument clear, dividing arguments into bullet points, finding simple ways to discuss complex ideas and making it clear when you are quoting others (lengthy quotations should be kept to a minimum: it is your ideas that the audience wants to hear, not the ideas of other researchers).

■ Prepare your visual aids and/or use presentation software (see 'Using Visual Aids', below).

■ Anticipate questions and rehearse answers.

- Anticipate criticisms so that you can rehearse arguments and prepare a defence of your ideas (engaging in this type of thesis defence will help to prepare you for your viva: see Chapter 23).

Presenting Your Paper

Give your technology requirements to the conference organizer before the conference takes place. Check that these have been met when you arrive. Try to view the room before you present your paper. You can check that all the required equipment and seating are available, and this should help you to relax a little. If you have to use a microphone, make sure that it is properly adjusted to your height before you begin speaking.

Make eye contact with members of the audience while you give your presentation (if it's a large audience, sweep your eyes across the room from time to time to show that you are including everyone). Don't be put off by people tweeting or using laptops and tablets. Maintain a good posture, relax and breathe quietly and deeply. Have a glass of water with you, if possible.

Let your audience know whether you are happy to receive questions during, or after, your presentation. Answer all questions with courtesy and respect. If you have anticipated questions correctly you should not be met with too many surprises. Also, you need to decide whether you wish to ask delegates to refrain from live tweeting during your presentation (some conferences outlaw this practice, others leave it to individual speakers and others encourage the practice by providing a live Twitter wall: see 'Twitter Wall' box, below).

Tip Make sure that your audience is able to take away a hard copy of your paper (your original, written version) if they have not been given a copy in the conference proceedings. This should include your name, department, university and contact details.

Using Visual Aids

Visual aids should be used in your presentation, if relevant. They add interest and help to explain and illustrate the points that you are making. They also help to keep your audience's attention.

When using visual aids, you should take note of the following:

- Make sure that text is clear and large enough so that it can be read by all members of the audience. This is of particular importance if using overhead projector transparencies, for example. Pay close attention to spelling, punctuation and grammar.

- If you are using photographs, pictures or slides, make sure that all images are clear enough to be seen by everybody. All sources must be fully acknowledged.

- Practise with all equipment prior to your presentation. Make sure that batteries/electric sockets are available and that your equipment is working. Have back-up visual aids available to cover unforeseen problems on the day.

Twitter Walls

Some conferences now have live Twitter walls (screens displaying live tweets) that allow delegates to discuss the presentation they are watching and enable other Twitter users to participate in the conference. Unfortunately, the use of Twitter walls can sometimes backfire, with rude or funny tweets making delegates laugh and putting off the speaker. Find out if such devices are to be used and anticipate any problems that could arise.

Using Presentation Software

If you want to use presentation software, contact your college/ university IT services or speak to your supervisor to find out what software is available for your use. Some colleges and universities run training courses on how to use the software, and others have online tutorials available. Software enables you to produce professional presentations, work together with others, organize and share your ideas, secure your work and measure the success of your presentation.

If you are interested in presentation software, you may find the following websites useful:

- SlideRocket (www.sliderocket.com);
- Prezi (http://prezi.com);
- Empressr (www.empressr.com);
- Vcasmo (http://vcasmo.com);
- PowerPoint (http://office.microsoft.com/powerpoint)

Summary

It is important for all advanced researchers to present papers at conferences. Doing so will enable you to improve your ideas and arguments, gain feedback from experts in your field and gain valuable presentation experience that can help in your future career. It is important to find the right conference and understand the requirements in terms of the type of paper, type of presentation and type of audience. If you are new to presenting at conferences you should seek further advice from your supervisor.

This section of the book has provided information and advice about disseminating the results of your research. When presenting research findings it is important to consider your participants, and issues of anonymity and confidentiality. This is part of being an ethical researcher and these issues are discussed in the following chapter.

27 Being an Ethical Researcher

All research activity must be carried out in an ethical manner. Funding organizations and university departments will want to know that you are aware of, and have addressed, the ethical aspects of your research. Also, other researchers, when reviewing and critiquing your work, will want to see that these issues have been addressed.

It is important to treat all participants with fairness and respect if you want people to continue volunteering for research projects in the future. It is also important to understand issues of confidentiality and anonymity, and know when your research proposal will need to be passed by your university ethics committee. These issues are discussed in this chapter.

Acting Ethically When Conducting Research

All advanced social researchers must act ethically in the following ways:

■ You must act ethically within the aims of research, which is to discover knowledge and avoid error. Acting ethically means you must not fabricate, falsify or misrepresent data.

- You must act ethically when you collaborate and cooperate with other researchers/academics. You must be trustworthy and accountable, and must act with mutual respect and fairness (this includes issues such as copyright, patents, data protection, plagiarism and intellectual property, for example).

- You must act ethically within established moral and social values (for example, you must adhere to health and safety rules, comply with the law, pay close regard to human rights and animal welfare, and avoid discrimination).

- You must act ethically when dealing with funding bodies. Research is more likely to be supported and funded if researchers are seen to be accountable and act with integrity.

- You must act ethically when dealing with the wider public. You must strive to promote social good and take action to mitigate social harms through your research.

- You must act ethically when working with research participants/subjects. You must treat them with dignity, privacy and autonomy, minimize harm and risk, and consider issues of informed consent and data protection (see Chapter 16).

- You must act ethically when publishing and disseminating results. This involves issues of confidentiality and anonymity, in addition to respecting the wishes and rights of those who have taken part in the research.

Tip The British Sociological Association has a 'Statement of Ethical Practice' that can be downloaded in full from its website: www.britsoc.co.uk. This is a comprehensive statement that covers issues such as professional integrity, relationships with research participants, anonymity, confidentiality, privacy and obligations to sponsors and funders. You can also download a working party report called 'Ethical Guidelines', which has been produced by the Social Research Association (http://the-sra.org.uk). This is a full and comprehensive guide that covers all ethical issues for social researchers.

Obtaining Funding and Ethics

Most reputable funding organizations will only fund research that meets their ethical criteria. These will be displayed on websites, sent with grant application forms or made available on request. When submitting a grant proposal you will need to demonstrate that you are aware of, and have addressed, all the ethical implications associated with your research (see Chapter 7 for more information about obtaining funding for your research).

Also, when applying for funding, you should only use reputable funding organizations that act ethically. Your university will have strict rules about the origins of research funding and, if there is any doubt, your proposal will need to be put before the ethics committee (or institutional review board in the United States).

In light of recent high-profile cases (such as funding that originated from the Gaddafi regime in Libya and from cigarette companies), many universities now require all applications for outside funding to be taken to the ethics committee for approval. Further advice can be obtained from your supervisor and university ethics committee.

Tip The Economic and Social Research Council (ESRC) has a document called the 'ESRC Framework for Research Ethics', which lays out the principles, procedures and minimum requirements for all types of research supported by the ESRC. A copy of the document can be downloaded from the ESRC website: www.esrc.ac.uk/about-esrc/information/research-ethics.aspx.

Treating Participants with Respect

All participants should be treated with respect and nobody should be exploited, bullied or cajoled into taking part in research or offering an opinion.

Taking part in research can affect people in different ways. Some people may find participation a rewarding process, whereas others will not. Your research should not give rise to false hopes or cause unnecessary anxiety. You must try to minimize the disruption to people's lives, and if someone has found it an upsetting experience you should find out why and try to ensure that the same situation does not occur again.

Some of the people who take part in your research may be vulnerable because of their age, social status or position of powerlessness. If participants are young, you need to make sure that a parent or guardian is present. If participants are ill or reaching old age, you might need to use a proxy and care must be taken to ensure that you do not affect the relationship between the proxy and the participant.

Ensuring Anonymity and Confidentiality

You must do your best to ensure anonymity and confidentiality. To ensure anonymity you need to show that you are taking steps to make sure that what participants have said cannot be traced back to them when you disseminate your results. You need to demonstrate how you intend to categorize and store information, and show how you are going to make sure that the information is not easily accessible to third parties. Also, participants need to know that what they say cannot be used against them in the future.

To ensure confidentiality you need to show that information supplied to you in confidence will not be disclosed directly to third parties. If the information is obtained in a group setting, issues of confidentiality should be relevant to the whole group (each member will need to agree not to disclose information directly to third parties). Again, you need to demonstrate how you are going to categorize and store the information so that it is kept safe and secure (see Chapter 16 for information about data protection legislation).

Tip   Information given by research participants in confidence does not enjoy legal privilege. This means that the information may be liable to subpoena by a court. If you are dealing with very sensitive information that you know could be called upon by a court of law, you will need to inform your participants that you would be obliged to hand over your data.

Conducting Research that Involves Risk

If your research involves any of the following types of risk you should seek further advice and clarification from your university research ethics committee or institutional review board. Some universities insist that this type of research is assessed by the ethics committee before it can go ahead (if in doubt, seek advice from your supervisor):

- research involving sensitive topics (e.g. sexual behaviour, violent behaviour, illegal behaviour, abuse or exploitation);
- research involving vulnerable groups (e.g. children and young people, those with a learning disability or cognitive impairment, individuals in an unequal power relationship);
- covert research that involves deception (e.g. the participants are unaware of your purpose and/or participants have not given informed consent);
- research that involves access to personal and confidential records;
- research that can cause psychological stress, anxiety or humiliation;
- research that may require the researcher to take part in, or observe, illegal behaviour;
- research that involves intrusive interventions (e.g. vigorous exercise, the administration of drugs or alternative therapies);
- research that requires you to get involved through an initial gatekeeper who may hold influence or power over those you seek to research.

Summary

It is important to act ethically throughout your research project, from developing your aims and objectives to obtaining funding, collecting data and reporting your results. You should be honest and act with integrity, treating colleagues and participants with respect and courtesy. You must carry out your research fairly and to the best of your ability, making sure that results are not misleading or falsified. You also have a responsibility to promote social good, avoid discrimination and adhere to relevant laws and institutional governance. If you take note of all this advice you can avoid ethical lapses that can cause harm to your personal reputation and to others.

This book has provided information about undertaking and completing an advanced research project. If you take note of the information and advice offered, and read around the relevant subject areas, you will be able to work through each stage of your project and achieve successful completion. I wish you every success in your research project and in your future research career.

Glossary of Terms

Action research

Action research is an interactive inquiry process (between researcher and participants) that moves forward to solve problems, improve practice or develop strategies. It moves beyond reflective knowledge, using empirical methods to develop well-informed action. Research methods that can be used in an action research project include interviews, focus groups, personal diaries and questionnaires.

Comparative analysis

Comparative analysis is a method that is used to analyse qualitative data. It is used to identify, analyse and explain similarities across groups, societies, institutions and cultures. Researchers can compare and contrast theories, schools of thought, case studies, historical personalities or literary texts, for example.

Constructionism

Constructionism is a social theory (or epistemological belief) that suggests that knowledge is constructed by scientists and not discovered from the world. The only reality that we know is that which is expressed by human thought. Meaning and knowledge are human constructions, and people construct these in different ways. Constructionism highlights the importance of culture and society on our construction of meaning and knowledge.

Content analysis

Content analysis is used in qualitative research to provide an objective, systematic and quantified description of the data. Using this method the researcher works through textual data identifying, coding and counting the presence of certain words, phrases, themes, characters or sentences, for example.

Conversation analysis

Conversation analysis is the study of social interaction within conversation. The focus is on the construction of reality, rather than the discovery of reality. Researchers are interested in understanding how participants interact with each other, how they contribute during interactions and how they make sense of the contributions that others make during the interaction.

Deconstruction

Deconstruction can be seen as a philosophical or literary criticism that questions traditional assumptions about certainty, identity and truth by delving below surface meaning. It challenges fundamental conceptual distinctions or oppositions in texts (for example, nature and culture, speech and writing, mind and body).

Deconstructive analysis

Deconstructive analysis is a technique of literary analysis that strips away multiple levels of meaning in a text to identify alternative explanations and meanings. It is suspicious of established intellectual categories and sceptical of claims to objectivity. Deconstructive analysis exposes contradictions and binary opposites in texts through taking apart the structure of language. It considers the multiple meanings of keywords in a text and the etymological relationship between words to understand how the text speaks with multiple voices.

Descriptive statistics

Descriptive statistics are used to describe and summarize data about the population that is under study, and to present data in a manageable form. They include measures of central tendencies (e.g. mean, median and mode), and measures of the variability or dispersion about the average (e.g. standard deviation or variance). These statistics are used to describe the basic features of the data in a study but cannot be used to make generalizations.

Discourse analysis

Discourse analysis is a general term that is used to describe a number of different approaches to studying and analysing the uses of language. This can be written, vocal or sign language, for example. Different approaches include semiotics, deconstruction and narrative analysis. Discourse analysis involves an interpretative and deconstructive reading of text but does not provide definitive answers.

Discourse theory

Discourse theory suggests that textual deep structures have a semantic rather than a syntactic character. It seeks to determine the universal semantic meaning of a text and display that meaning in the form of concepts, propositions and paragraphs, for example, and their relationship to one another. Discourse theory is used to build on existing knowledge and is subject to continuous debate and argument. It does not seek to provide specific answers to a problem.

Epistemology

Epistemology is a branch of philosophy that studies the nature of knowledge. It considers the presumptions that underpin knowledge and the foundations on which knowledge is built, investigating issues such as the origin, nature, methods and limits of human knowledge. It refers to what we accept as knowledge, how we know what we know and how belief is justified.

Ethnography

Ethnography is the study and systematic recording (and reporting) of human cultures and human societies. The emphasis in ethnography is on describing and interpreting cultural behaviour and phenomena from the point of view of the subject rather than the ethnographer. Studies concentrate on the detail of day-to-day lives to provide insight into social and cultural phenomena, through such methods as participant observation, comparative fieldwork and interviews.

Experimental research

Commonly referred to as the 'scientific method', experimental research can be viewed as both a methodology and a method. This type of research seeks to add to knowledge through diligent inquiry that involves systematic and controlled testing to understand causal processes. Researchers manipulate one or more variables, controlling and measuring changes in other variables. They also examine data, reports and observations in the search for facts or principles.

Feminist empiricism

Feminist empiricism seeks to discover a more objective truth by eliminating such biases as gender, class and race from the research process. Traditional Western scholarship and science are seen to have been developed purely from a white, male, middle-class perspective, and research has been conducted from this standpoint, eliminating or belittling the experiences of 'subordinate' groups. Feminist empiricism seeks to redress the balance.

Feminist postmodernism

Feminist postmodernism suggests that there is no single truth that can be researched and reported, as women's experiences vary according to age, race, class, culture, sexual orientation, education and other variables. It recognizes that there are multiple explanations of reality. It is important to look for the basic social process that leads to variations in behaviour within the conditions imposed by the existing structure of society.

Feminist research

Feminist researchers argue that for too long the lives and experiences of women have been ignored or misrepresented. Feminist researchers critique both the research topics and the methods used, especially those that emphasize objective, scientific 'truth'. With its emphasis on participative, qualitative inquiry, feminist research has provided a valuable alternative framework for researchers who have felt uncomfortable with treating people as research 'objects'.

Feminist standpoint research

Feminist standpoint research suggests that knowledge is shaped by the social context of the knower. As knowledge is constructed from the position of the knower, science is part of the social order and is viewed and produced exclusively by the powerful in society. Therefore, previous problems with 'masculine' science can be counteracted by taking the lives and experiences of women as the starting point for any knowledge production.

Full Economic Costing

Full Economic Costing (fEC) is a government initiative that requires universities to cost research activities based on direct and indirect costs, which include space/estates charges and depreciation. The initiative was introduced to help universities recover a greater proportion of the true costs of research and to ensure adequate recurring investment in university infrastructure. The abbreviation fEC is used rather than FEC (recognized as referring to Further Education Colleges).

Gold open access

Gold open access publishing is a method of publishing where the author publishes in an open access journal, but the article is only made available on payment of a publication or processing fee. This fee tends to be paid by the author's institution or funding body (the cost of the fee is included in the grant proposal).

Grounded theory

Grounded theory was described in 1967 by Glaser and Strauss. It is a systematic qualitative methodology used in the social sciences to generate theory that is grounded in the data. The researcher begins by collecting data using a variety of methods, and then works through a series of stages. This includes coding, grouping codes into concepts, developing concepts into categories and using categories as a basis for theory generation. Literature is reviewed throughout the process to help to explain emerging categories and concepts.

Heuristic inquiry

Heuristic inquiry is an adaptation of phenomenological inquiry. Instead of putting aside preconceptions, however, the researcher acknowledges their involvement, to the extent that the lived experience of the researcher becomes one of the main focuses of the research. Heuristic inquiry searches for essential meanings connected with everyday human experiences. Imagination, intuition and self-reflection are important aspects of this approach.

Inferential statistics

Inferential statistics are used by researchers to analyse samples and draw conclusions. They help deductions to be made from the data collected and enable the researcher to test hypotheses and relate findings to the sample or population. Tests of significance are used to address issues of generalizability. Inferential statistics can be used to make predictions about what might happen in the future.

Methodology

Methodology is a guideline system or framework that is used for solving a problem. It includes practices, procedures and rules used by those involved in inquiry and covers issues such as the constraints, dilemmas and ethical choices within social research. It also includes the theoretical analysis of these systems or frameworks, a critique of other frameworks and a careful analysis of the interrelationship between epistemological standpoint, theoretical perspective and methodology.

Narrative analysis

Narrative analysis (or narrative inquiry) is a type of qualitative technique that focuses on how people construct and use stories to interpret the world. These stories can be in the form of conversations, interviews, field notes, letters, journals, autobiographies and life histories, for example. The narratives are seen as interpretative devices through which people represent themselves and their social worlds to others.

Non-probability samples

A non-probability sample is a method of sampling that is used when description rather than generalization is the goal. In this type of sample it is not possible to specify the possibility of one person being included in the sample. Instead, the sample is selected on the basis of knowledge of the research problem. There are various types of non-probability sample, including quota samples, judgemental samples and convenience samples.

Objectivism

Objectivism is an epistemological belief that highlights the importance of empirical facts and explicit articulate statements. Reality exists independently of consciousness and objective knowledge can be obtained through experience, observation and deductive reasoning. Objectivists believe that truth is determined through the use of the scientific method (replicable observations represent the truth). Observations are neutral, scientific knowledge connects directly with reality and knowledge is value-free.

Phenomenological research

Phenomenology is the study of the nature and meanings of phenomena. The aim is to understand, interpret and describe the structure of lived experience, or the 'life-world', rather than explain it. In phenomenological research the main data collection method is the interview, which is used to focus on a participant's perception of lived experience. Data analysis involves a search for all possible meanings and an in-depth analysis of specific statements and themes. It is important for the researcher to set aside all prejudgements.

Positivism

Positivism is a philosophy of science that suggests that empirical sciences are the sole source of true knowledge. The purpose of science is to observe and measure so that we can find the truth, understand the world and make predictions. Through using the scientific method (experimentation, deductive reasoning and hypothesis development and testing) we can come to understand the laws of cause and effect.

Postmodernism

Postmodernism suggests that there is no single defining source for truth and reality beyond the individual. It is not possible to obtain one particular view of the world; instead, there are numerous views found through the interpretation or deconstruction of existing concepts, belief systems or generally held social values and assumptions. Postmodernism emphasizes concrete experience over abstract principles.

Post-positivism

Post-positivism suggests that although objective truth is there to be sought, the researcher can influence what is observed. It suggests that all observation is fallible and can contain errors, and all theory is revisable and can be improved upon. Objectivity cannot be found in individual scientists, but is a social phenomenon that can be worked towards through careful experimentation, triangulation, academic scrutiny and theoretical criticism.

Post-structuralism

Post-structuralism suggests that meanings and intellectual categories are shifting and unstable. What an author means is only secondary to what the reader perceives, and what a reader perceives varies, depending on identity (race, class, gender, etc.). Human sciences are unstable because human beings are complex and it is impossible for researchers to break free of social structures when studying them.

Probability samples

A probability sample is a method of sampling that uses some form of random selection. It is used when the researcher wants to ensure that all people within the study population have a specifiable chance of being selected. This type of sample is used if the researcher wishes to explain, predict or generalize to the whole research population. Since the sample serves as a model for the whole research population, it must be an accurate representation of this population. There are different types of probability sample, including simple random samples, cluster samples and stratified random samples.

Reliability

Reliability is concerned with the way that a research instrument is able to yield the same results in repeated trials. It refers to consistency of measurement and asks whether other researchers would get the same results under the same conditions. Replication of statistically significant results is essential if the scientific community is to accept research findings and establish them as scientific truth. Issues of reliability are fundamental to the scientific method.

Repository-based green open access publishing

Repository-based green open access publishing is where the author publishes in a journal and then self-archives an unformatted/pre-print copy in an institutional or subject-based repository. Many higher education institutions now require that all articles and conference papers are deposited in their repository (with a voluntary deposit of book chapters and monographs, if publisher permission is sought). Repository members of staff are available to help with deposits and check issues of copyright.

Semiotics

Semiotics is a type of discourse analysis that focuses on how signs and symbols are interpreted, used and create meaning. There are three areas of study: semantics, which looks at the relationship between the signs and that to which they refer; syntactics, which looks at the relationship of signs to their formal structures; and pragmatics, which considers the relationships between signs and the effects that they have on people who use them.

Subjectivism

Subjectivism is a social theory (or epistemological belief) that suggests that there is no underlying truth and that reality is only what we perceive it to be. Knowledge and truth are created, not discovered, and as such knowledge cannot be value-free. All knowledge is limited to experiences by the self and transcendent knowledge is impossible. Therefore, knowledge cannot be discovered as it is subjectively acquired and everything is relative.

Survey research

Survey research is a quantitative methodology that can be used for exploratory purposes, to test theory and to understand and describe a particular phenomenon, for example. The methodology is used to gather data about thoughts, opinions, attitudes, behaviour and feelings. Respondents are asked a set of pre-defined questions using methods such as questionnaires or structured interviews (by mail, telephone, internet or face-to-face, for example).

Symbolic interactionism

Symbolic interactionism is a social theory that suggests that behaviour is explained in terms of how people interact with each other via symbols. It suggests that reality exists but is developed through social interaction (society and individuals cannot be separated from one another). Symbolic interactionism is concerned with the analyses of patterns of communication, interpretation, interaction and adjustment between individuals.

Thematic analysis

Thematic analysis is a method of data analysis used in qualitative research to identify specific themes (clusters of linked categories that convey similar meanings, which are related to the research question). These categories are coded, counted, altered and modified in light of new data. Analysis can continue into the writing-up process because themes can be modified and tightened during this process.

Validity

Issues of validity are fundamental to the scientific method. Validity refers to the accuracy of the measurement, and asks whether the tests that a researcher undertakes are measuring what they are supposed to measure. There are different types of validity, including face validity (the appearance of the questions), content validity (reflecting the subject of the research) and construct validity (assessing the theoretical concept).

Viva voce

A viva voce (or viva) is an oral examination that is used to test a student's knowledge (and defence) of their thesis. It is mostly used at doctoral level, although some undergraduate and Master's students can be called to attend a viva. The panel usually consists of one or two internal examiners and an external examiner. During a viva a student should be able to demonstrate their ability to enter into academic discussion with research colleagues.

References, Further Reading and Resources

Chapter 1: Understanding the Epistemological Debate

References

Crotty, M., *The Foundations of Social Science Research: Meaning and Perspective in the Research Process* (New South Wales: Allen and Unwin, 1998).

Further Reading

Audi, R., *Epistemology: A Contemporary Introduction to the Theory of Knowledge* (3rd edition, New York, NY: Routledge, 2011).

Harding, S. and M. Hintikka (eds), *Discovering Reality: Feminist Perspectives on Epistemology, Metaphysics, Methodology, and Philosophy of Science* (Dordrecht: Kluwer Academic Publishers, 2003).

O'Brien, D., *An Introduction to the Theory of Knowledge* (Cambridge: Polity Press, 2006).

Chapter 2: Understanding the Methodological Debate

References

Crotty, M., *The Foundations of Social Science Research: Meaning and Perspective in the Research Process* (New South Wales: Allen and Unwin, 1998).

Glaser, B. and A. Strauss, *The Discovery of Grounded Theory* (Chicago, IL: Aldine, 1967).

Griffin, C., 'Feminism, Social Psychology and Qualitative Research', *Psychologist*, 8: 3 (1995), 119–21.

Harding, S., *Whose Science? Whose Knowledge? Thinking From Women's Lives* (Milton Keynes: Open University Press, 1991).

Wuest, J., 'Feminist Grounded Theory – An Exploration of the Congruency and Tensions Between Two Traditions in Knowledge Discovery', *Qualitative Health Research*, 5: 1 (1995), 125–37.

Further Reading

Clough, P. and C. Nutbrown, *A Student's Guide to Methodology* (3rd edition, London: Sage, 2012).

Flick, U., *Designing Qualitative Research* (London: Sage, 2007).

Kumar, R., *Research Methodology: A Step-by-Step Guide for Beginners* (3rd edition, London: Sage, 2011).

Letherby, G., J. Scott and M. Williams, *Objectivity and Subjectivity in Social Research* (London: Sage, 2013).

Silverman, D., *Doing Qualitative Research* (3rd edition, London: Sage, 2010).

Chapter 3: Generating Ideas

Further Reading

White, P., *Developing Research Questions: A Guide for Social Scientists* (London: Palgrave Macmillan, 2009).

Chapter 4: Justifying Your Research

Further Reading

Creswell, J., *Qualitative Inquiry and Research Design: Choosing Among Five Approaches* (3rd edition, Thousand Oaks, CA: Sage, 2013).

Haack, S., *Defending Science, Within Reason: Between Scientism and Cynicism* (New York, NY: Prometheus Books, 2007).

Porta, D. and M. Keating, *Approaches and Methodologies in the Social Sciences: A Pluralist Perspective* (New York, NY: Cambridge University Press, 2008).

Chapter 7: Obtaining Funding

Further Reading

Aldridge, J. and A. Derrington, *The Research Funding Toolkit: How to Plan and Write Successful Grant Applications* (London: Sage, 2012).

Berry, D., *Gaining Funding for Research: A Guide for Academics and Institutions* (Maidenhead: Open University Press, 2010).

Useful Websites

Research Professional (www.researchprofessional.com) provides information about research-based funding opportunities and news about research policy in the UK. You can use the public website (www.researchresearch.com) to find out more about the organization, but you will need to subscribe to access information about specific funding opportunities (most universities subscribe to the service).

Euraxess Funding Search (http://euraxessfunds.britishcouncil.org) is provided by the British Council and is a searchable database that enables researchers to obtain funding for international travel, short research visits and overseas fellowships (for researchers coming from and to the UK).

Foundation Center (http://foundationcenter.org) offers basic information on funding organizations in the United States. This includes private foundations, community foundations, grant-making public charities and corporate giving programmes.

Chapter 8: Collecting Background Information

Further Reading

Hock, R., *The Extreme Searcher's Internet Handbook: A Guide for the Serious Searcher* (4th edition, Medford, NJ: Information Today, 2013).

Chapter 9: Choosing Research Methods

References

Crotty, M., *The Foundations of Social Science Research: Meaning and Perspective in the Research Process* (New South Wales: Allen and Unwin, 1998).

Further Reading

Bryman, A., *Social Research Methods* (4th edition, Oxford: Oxford University Press, 2012).

Cohen, L., L. Manion and K. Morrison, *Research Methods in Education* (7th edition, Abingdon: Routledge, 2011).

Henn, M., M. Weinstein and N. Foard, *A Critical Introduction to Social Research* (2nd edition, London: Sage, 2009).

Letherby, G., *Feminist Research in Theory and Practice* (Buckingham: Open University Press, 2003).

Robson, C., *Real World Research* (3rd edition, Chichester: John Wiley and Sons, 2011).

Chapter 10: Understanding Sampling Techniques

Further Reading

Andres, L., *Designing and Doing Survey Research* (London: Sage, 2012).

Henry, G., *Practical Sampling* (Newbury Park, CA: Sage, 1990).

Chapter 11: Producing a Research Proposal

Further Reading

Punch, K., *Developing Effective Research Proposals* (2nd edition, London: Sage, 2006).

Chapter 12: Running Focus Groups

References

Madriz, E., 'Focus Groups in Feminist Research', in N. Denzin and Y. Lincoln (eds), *Collecting and Interpreting Qualitative Materials* (Thousand Oaks, CA: Sage, 2003).

Further Reading

Barbour, R., *Doing Focus Groups* (London: Sage, 2007).

Liamputtong, P., *Focus Group Methodology* (London: Sage, 2011).

Chapter 13: Conducting Interviews

Further Reading

Gillham, B., *Research Interviewing: The Range of Techniques* (Maidenhead: Open University Press, 2005).

Gubrium, J. and J. Holstein (eds), *Postmodern Interviewing* (Thousand Oaks, CA: Sage, 2003).

Kvale, S., *Doing Interviews* (London: Sage, 2007).

Kvale, S. and S. Brinkmann, *InterViews: Learning the Craft of Qualitative Research Interviewing* (2nd edition, Thousand Oaks, CA: Sage, 2009).

Seidman, I., *Interviewing as Qualitative Research: A Guide for Researchers in Education and the Social Sciences* (4th edition, New York, NY: Teachers College Press, 2013).

Chapter 14: Using Questionnaires

Further Reading

Andres, L., *Designing and Doing Survey Research* (London: Sage, 2012).

Blair, J., R. Czaja and E. Blair, *Designing Surveys: A Guide to Decisions and Procedures* (3rd edition, Thousand Oaks, CA: Sage, 2013).

Gillham, B., *Developing a Questionnaire* (2nd edition, London: Continuum, 2007).

Chapter 15: Becoming a Participant Observer

Further Reading

Angrosino, M. *Doing Ethnographic and Observational Research* (London: Sage, 2007).

Aull Davies, C. *Reflexive Ethnography: A Guide to Researching Selves and Others* (2nd edition, New York: Routledge, 2007).

DeWalt, K. and B. DeWalt, *Participant Observation: A Guide for Fieldworkers* (2nd edition, Lanham, MD: AltaMira Press, 2011).

Chapter 16: Recording and Storing Data

Further Reading

Duncan, G., M. Elliot and G. Salazar, *Statistical Confidentiality: Principles and Practice* (New York, NY: Springer, 2013).

Social Research Association, *Data Protection Act 1998: Guidelines*.

Chapter 17: Using the Internet

Further Reading

Baym, N., *Personal Connections in the Digital Age* (Cambridge: Polity, 2010).

Hooley, T., J. Wellens and J. Marriott, *What is Online Research? Using the Internet for Social Research* (London: Bloomsbury Academic, 2012).

McKee, H. and J. Porter, *The Ethics of Internet Research: A Rhetorical, Case-based Process* (New York, NY: Peter Lang, 2009).

Thelwall, M, *Introduction to Webometrics: Quantitative Web Research for the Social Sciences* (San Rafael, CA: Morgan and Claypool, 2009).

Chapter 18: Understanding Qualitative Techniques

Further Reading

Gibbs, G., *Analysing Qualitative Data* (London: Sage, 2007).

Glaser, B. and A. Strauss, *The Discovery of Grounded Theory* (Chicago, IL: Aldine, 1967).

Guest, G., K. MacQueen and E. Namey, *Applied Thematic Analysis* (Thousand Oaks, CA: Sage, 2012).

Hahn, C., *Doing Qualitative Research Using Your Computer: A Practical Guide* (London: Sage, 2008).

Krippendorff, K., *Content Analysis: An Introduction to its Methodology* (3rd edition, London: Sage, 2012).

Ragin, C., *The Comparative Method: Moving Beyond Qualitative and Quantitative Strategies* (Berkeley, CA: University of California Press, 1987).

Richards, L., *Handling Qualitative Data: A Practical Guide* (London: Sage, 2009).

Saldaña, J., *The Coding Manual For Social Researchers* (London: Sage, 2009).

Sidnell, J., *Conversation Analysis: An Introduction* (Chichester: Wiley-Blackwell, 2010).

Silverman, D., *Interpreting Qualitative Data* (4th edition, London: Sage, 2011).

Wetherell, M., S. Taylor and S. Yates (eds), *Discourse as Data: A Guide to Analysis* (London: Sage, 2001).

Wooffitt, R., *Conversation Analysis and Discourse Analysis: A Comparative and Critical Introduction* (London: Sage, 2005).

Chapter 19: Understanding Quantitative Techniques

Further Reading

Bickman, L. and D. Rog (eds), *The Sage Handbook of Applied Social Research Methods* (2nd edition, Thousand Oaks, CA: Sage, 2008).

Blaikie, N., *Analyzing Quantitative Data: From Description to Explanation* (London: Sage, 2003).

Caldwell, S., *Statistics Unplugged* (4th edition, Belmont, CA: Cengage Learning, 2013).

Elliot, J. and C. Marsh, *Exploring Data: An Introduction to Data Analysis for Social Scientists* (2nd edition, Cambridge: Polity Press, 2008).

Hardy, M. and A. Bryman, *Handbook of Data Analysis* (London: Sage, 2009).

Rowntree, D., *Statistics Without Tears: An Introduction for Non-Mathematicians* (London: Penguin, 2000).

Chapter 20: Interpreting and Critiquing Data

Further Reading

Byrne, D., *Interpreting Quantitative Data* (London: Sage, 2002).

Silverman, D., *Interpreting Qualitative Data* (4th edition, London: Sage, 2011).

Chapter 21: Developing Theory

Further Reading

Inglis, D. and C. Thorpe, *An Invitation to Social Theory* (Cambridge: Polity Press, 2012).

Layder, D., *Understanding Social Theory* (2nd edition, London: Sage, 2005).

Chapter 22: Producing Your Thesis

Further Reading

Murray, R., *How to Write a Thesis* (3rd edition, Maidenhead: Open University Press, 2011).

Chapter 23: Passing Your Viva

Further Reading

Murray, R., *How to Survive your Viva: Defending a Thesis in an Oral Examination* (2nd edition, Maidenhead: Open University Press, 2009).

Rugg, G. and M. Petre, *The Unwritten Rules of PhD Research* (Maidenhead: Open University Press, 2004).

Wellington, J., A. Bathmaker, C. Hunt and G. McCulloch, *Succeeding with Your Doctorate* (London: Sage, 2005).

Chapter 24: Writing Journal Articles

Further Reading

Murray, R., *Writing for Academic Journals* (Maidenhead: Open University Press, 2009).

Chapter 25: Publishing Online

Useful Resources

The Registry of Open Access Repositories (ROAR) is hosted by the University of Southampton (http://roar.eprints.org). Its aim is to promote the development of open access by providing information about the growth and status of repositories throughout the world. Visit the website to find out more about the registry and to search for articles using search terms such as content, country and type of repository.

The Registry of Open Access Repositories Mandatory Archiving Policies (ROARMAP) is a companion database to ROAR, also produced by the University of Southampton (http://roarmap.eprints.org). You can browse the database by country and by repository type.

The Directory of Open Access Journals (http://www.doaj.org) has been set up to increase the visibility and use of open access scientific and scholarly journals. This site offers free online access to high-quality content, and provides useful quick and advanced search facilities to help you find relevant articles. You can also export references to referencing software such as Reference Manager (http://www.refman.com) and EndNote (http://endnote.com), which saves considerable time when producing references and bibliographies.

Chapter 26: Presenting at Conferences

Further Reading

Malmfors, B., P. Garnsworthy and M. Grossman, *Writing and Presenting Scientific Papers* (2nd edition, Nottingham: Nottingham University Press, 2004).

Shephard, K., *Presenting at Conferences, Seminars and Meetings* (London: Sage, 2005).

Chapter 27: Being an Ethical Researcher

Further Reading

Hammersley, M. and A. Traianou, *Ethics in Qualitative Research: Controversies and Contexts* (London: Sage, 2012).

Miller, T., M. Birch, M. Mauthner and J. Jessop (eds), *Ethics in Qualitative Research* (2nd edition, London: Sage, 2012).

Ransome, P., *Ethics and Values in Social Research* (London: Palgrave Macmillan, 2013).

Bibliography

Aldridge, J. and A. Derrington, *The Research Funding Toolkit: How to Plan and Write Successful Grant Applications* (London: Sage, 2012).

Andres, L., *Designing and Doing Survey Research* (London: Sage, 2012).

Angrosino, M., *Doing Ethnographic and Observational Research* (London: Sage, 2007).

Audi, R., *Epistemology: A Contemporary Introduction to the Theory of Knowledge* (3rd edition, New York, NY: Routledge, 2011).

Aull Davies, C., *Reflexive Ethnography: A Guide to Researching Selves and Others* (2nd edition, New York, NY: Routledge, 2007).

Barbour, R., *Doing Focus Groups* (London: Sage, 2007).

Baym, R., *Personal Connections in the Digital Age* (Cambridge: Polity, 2010).

Berry, D., *Gaining Funding for Research: A Guide for Academics and Institutions* (Maidenhead: Open University Press, 2010).

Bickman, L. and D. Rog (eds), *The Sage Handbook of Applied Social Research Methods* (2nd edition, Thousand Oaks, CA: Sage, 2008).

Blaikie, N., *Analyzing Quantitative Data: From Description to Explanation* (London: Sage, 2003).

Blair, J., R. Czaja and E. Blair, *Designing Surveys: A Guide to Decisions and Procedures* (3rd edition, Thousand Oaks, CA: Sage, 2013).

Bryman, A., *Social Research Methods* (4th edition, Oxford: Oxford University Press, 2012).

Byrne, D., *Interpreting Quantitative Data* (London: Sage, 2002).

Caldwell, S., *Statistics Unplugged* (4th edition, Belmont, CA: Cengage Learning, 2013).

Clough, P. and C. Nutbrown, *A Student's Guide to Methodology* (3rd edition, London: Sage, 2012).

Cohen, L., L. Manion and K. Morrison, *Research Methods in Education* (7th edition, Abingdon: Routledge, 2011).

Creswell, J., *Qualitative Inquiry and Research Design: Choosing Among Five Approaches* (3rd edition, Thousand Oaks, CA: Sage, 2013).

Crotty, M. *The Foundations of Social Science Research: Meaning and Perspective in the Research Process* (New South Wales: Allen and Unwin, 1998).

DeWalt, K. and B. DeWalt, *Participant Observation: A Guide for Fieldworkers* (2nd edition, Lanham, MD: AltaMira Press, 2011).

Duncan, G., M. Elliot and G. Salazar, *Statistical Confidentiality: Principles and Practice* (New York, NY: Springer, 2013).

Elliot, J. and C. Marsh, *Exploring Data: An Introduction to Data Analysis for Social Scientists* (2nd edition, Cambridge: Polity Press, 2008).

Flick, U., *Designing Qualitative Research* (London: Sage, 2007).

Gibbs, G., *Analysing Qualitative Data* (London: Sage, 2007).

Gillham, B., *Developing a Questionnaire* (2nd edition, London: Continuum, 2007).

—, *Research Interviewing: The Range of Techniques* (Maidenhead: Open University Press, 2005).

Glaser, B. and A. Strauss, *The Discovery of Grounded Theory* (Chicago, IL: Aldine, 1967).

Gubrium, J. and J. Holstein (eds), *Postmodern Interviewing* (Thousand Oaks, CA: Sage, 2003).

Guest, G., K. MacQueen and E. Namey, *Applied Thematic Analysis* (Thousand Oaks, CA: Sage, 2012).

Haack, S., *Defending Science, Within Reason: Between Scientism and Cynicism* (New York, NY: Prometheus Books, 2007).

Hammersley, M. and A. Traianou, *Ethics in Qualitative Research: Controversies and Contexts* (London: Sage, 2012).

Harding, S. and M. Hintikka (eds), *Discovering Reality: Feminist Perspectives on Epistemology, Metaphysics, Methodology, and Philosophy of Science* (Dordrecht: Kluwer Academic Publishers, 2003).

Hardy, M. and A. Bryman, *Handbook of Data Analysis* (London: Sage, 2009).

Henn, M., M. Weinstein and N. Foard, *A Critical Introduction to Social Research* (2nd edition, London: Sage, 2009).

Henry, G., *Practical Sampling* (Newbury Park, CA: Sage, 1990).

Hock, R., *The Extreme Searcher's Internet Handbook: A Guide for the Serious Searcher* (4th edition, Medford, NJ: Information Today, 2013).

Hooley, T., J. Wellens and J. Marriott, *What is Online Research? Using the Internet for Social Research* (London: Bloomsbury Academic, 2012).

Inglis, D. and C. Thorpe, *An Invitation to Social Theory* (Cambridge: Polity Press, 2012).

Kumar, R., *Research Methodology: A Step-by-Step Guide for Beginners* (3rd edition, London: Sage, 2011).

Kvale, S., *Doing Interviews* (London: Sage, 2007).

Kvale, S. and S. Brinkmann, *InterViews: Learning the Craft of Qualitative Research Interviewing* (2nd edition, Thousand Oaks, CA: Sage, 2009).

Layder, D., *Understanding Social Theory* (2nd edition, London: Sage, 2005).

Letherby, G., *Feminist Research in Theory and Practice* (Buckingham: Open University Press, 2003).

Letherby, G., J. Scott and M. Williams, *Objectivity and Subjectivity in Social Research* (London: Sage, 2013).

Malmfors, B., P. Garnsworthy and M. Grossman, *Writing and Presenting Scientific Papers* (2nd edition, Nottingham: Nottingham University Press, 2004).

McKee, H. and J. Porter, *The Ethics of Internet Research: A Rhetorical, Case-based Process* (New York, NY: Peter Lang, 2009).

Miller, T., M. Birch, M. Mauthner and J. Jessop (eds), *Ethics in Qualitative Research* (2nd edition, London: Sage, 2012).

Murray, R., *How to Survive Your Viva: Defending a Thesis in an Oral Examination* (2nd edition, Maidenhead: Open University Press, 2009).

—, *How to Write a Thesis* (3rd edition, Maidenhead: Open University Press, 2011).

—, *Writing for Academic Journals* (Maidenhead: Open University Press, 2009).

O'Brien, D., *An Introduction to the Theory of Knowledge* (Cambridge: Polity Press, 2006).

Porta, D. and M. Keating, *Approaches and Methodologies in the Social Sciences: A Pluralist Perspective* (New York, NY: Cambridge University Press, 2008).

Punch, K., *Developing Effective Research Proposals* (2nd edition, London: Sage, 2006).

Ransome, P., *Ethics and Values in Social Research* (London: Palgrave Macmillan, 2013).

Richards, L., *Handling Qualitative Data: A Practical Guide* (London: Sage, 2009).

Robson, C., *Real World Research* (3rd edition, Chichester: John Wiley and Sons, 2011).

Rowntree, D., *Statistics Without Tears: An Introduction for Non-Mathematicians* (London: Penguin, 2000).

Rugg, G. and M. Petre, *The Unwritten Rules of PhD Research* (Maidenhead: Open University Press, 2004).

Saldaña, J., *The Coding Manual for Social Researchers* (London: Sage, 2009).

Seidman, I., *Interviewing as Qualitative Research: A Guide for Researchers in Education and the Social Sciences* (4th edition, New York, NY: Teachers College Press, 2013).

Shephard, K., *Presenting at Conferences, Seminars and Meetings* (London: Sage, 2005).

Silverman, D., *Doing Qualitative Research* (3rd edition, London: Sage, 2010).

—, *Interpreting Qualitative Data* (4th edition, London: Sage, 2011).

Thelwall, M., *Introduction to Webometrics: Quantitative Web Research for the Social Sciences* (San Rafael, CA: Morgan and Claypool, 2009).

Wellington, J., A. Bathmaker, C. Hunt and G. McCulloch, *Succeeding with Your Doctorate* (London: Sage, 2005).

White, P., *Developing Research Questions: A Guide for Social Scientists* (London: Palgrave Macmillan, 2009).

Index